Praise for *The Fir...*

"Thoughtful storytelling . . . snappy writing. Kennedy . . . exposes a stirring tale of lost love (which could have been grist for its own book) in just the sort of smart read we've come to expect from her."
—*Boston Globe*

"Devastatingly good . . . Novelist Kennedy's literary chops serve her well in this fascinating and heartbreaking social history."
—*Booklist* (starred review)

"A well-sculpted account of Dillon's remarkable life amid the buttoned-up attitudes of her times. Kennedy splices in fascinating side stories associated with Dillon's saga . . . When Dillon began his quest . . . he struggled alone. Had his autobiography been published or he'd survived to live openly, Dillon could have been a model for others. Thanks to Kennedy, his story has finally been given a life."
—*San Francisco Chronicle*

"Absolutely outstanding. By far the best biography of a transgendered person that I have read."
—**Ben Barres, professor of neurobiology, Stanford University**

"This story is fascinating to modern readers whether or not they have personal questions about gender." —*School Library Journal*

"This book is pure brilliance—the research, the execution, the wonder and heartbreak. What an incredible story. What is it to be a human being? Who are we? Everyone should read this book as we stumble through our lives." —**Natalie Goldberg, author of** *Writing Down the Bones* **and** *The Great Failure*

THE FIRST MAN-MADE MAN

BY THE SAME AUTHOR

THE FIRST MAN-MADE MAN

The Story of Two Sex Changes,

One Love Affair, and a

Twentieth-Century

Medical Revolution

PAGAN KENNEDY

BLOOMSBURY

Photo credits: Photos 1 and 4: Courtesy of the British Association of Plastic
Surgeons. Photos 2 and 6: From the collection of Liz Hodgkinson.
Photos 7 and 10: Courtesy of the Hulton Archive. Photos 8 and 12: Courtesy of
The Kinsey Institute for Research in Sex, Gender and Reproduction.
Photo 13 and image 14: From Sangharakshita's private collection,
licensed by the Clear Vision Trust.

Published by Bloomsbury USA, New York
Distributed to the trade by Macmillan

All papers used by Bloomsbury USA are natural, recyclable products made
from wood grown in well-managed forests. The manufacturing processes
conform to the environmental regulations of the country of origin.

THE LIBRARY OF CONGRESS HAS CATALOGED THE HARDCOVER EDITION AS FOLLOWS:

Kennedy, Pagan, 1962–
The first man-made man : the story of two sexes, one love affair, and a
twentieth-century medical revolution / Pagan Kennedy.—1st U.S. ed.
p. cm.
ISBN-13: 978-1-59691-015-7 (hardcover)
ISBN-10: 1-59691-015-1 (hardcover)
1. Dillon, Michael, 1915–1962. 2. Transsexuals—Great Britain—Biography. 3. Sex
change—Great Britain—Biography. 4. Gender identity—Great Britain. I. Title.

HQ77.8.D55K46 2006
306.76'80941—dc22
2006018511

First published by Bloomsbury USA in 2007
This paperback edition published in 2008

Paperback ISBN-10: 1-59691-016-X
ISBN-13: 978-1-59691-016-4

1 3 5 7 9 10 8 6 4 2

Typeset by Westchester Book Group
Printed in the United States of America by Quebecor World Fairfield

CONTENTS

AUTHOR'S NOTE

In this book I often use the word *transsexual* rather than *transgendered* to refer to people who have switched sex. I do this because I am discussing a time in which the word *transgender* did not yet exist. In addition, *transsexual* tends to connote those who have used surgery and hormones to change their appearance—which is true of most of the people documented here. My use of the word *transsexual* is not intended to strike any particular political tone, but rather to avoid confusion.

Pronouns, too, caused me angst. For clarity, I often found it necessary to refer to Laura Dillon as "she" and Robert Cowell as "he," even though these pronouns did not match Dillon's or Cowell's internal sense of themselves before they transformed their bodies. Wherever possible, I have tried to use the pronoun that refers to a person's preferred gender role rather than his/her body type.

PART I
MAKE THE BODY

CHAPTER 1
HE PROPOSES

MICHAEL DILLON, A BEARDED MEDICAL STUDENT, fiddled with his pipe and then lit it nervously. The year was 1950; the city, London; the restaurant, discreet. Dillon shared his table with a person so odd-looking that the other diners in the restaurant ogled and whispered to one another. He—or was it a she?—wore a blazer and trousers, cropped hair, and tie, but seemed to be hiding breasts under the suit jacket. In fact, Roberta Cowell had been born male, but she could not live as a man anymore. She had begun dosing herself on massive amounts of estrogen—enough to melt away her muscles and put a blush in her cheeks. With no idea how to push her transformation further, Cowell was stuck in a no-man's-land between the sexes—a terrible place to find yourself in 1950.

The word *transsexual* had yet to enter common usage. Almost no medical literature acknowledged that thousands of people felt trapped in the wrong body and would do anything—including risk death—to change their sex. Michael Dillon, the medical student, had authored what was then one of the few books in the world to delve into the subject. In an eccentric little volume called *Self: A Study in Ethics and Endocrinology*, he had argued on behalf of people like Roberta Cowell. Dillon proposed an idea that seemed wildly radical at that time: why not give patients the body they wanted? Thanks to recent technological breakthroughs, doctors could transform a man into a woman and vice versa. But because of the stigma against these sex changes—as well as laws that prohibited castration—only a few people in the world had ever crossed the line.

Roberta Cowell had discovered Michael Dillon's book and decided she had to meet the open-minded scholar. She'd written to him care of his publisher and they'd exchanged a flurry of letters. Now, finally, they sat across from one another.

Dillon turned out to be handsome, Cowell reported in her autobiography. "He was a good deal younger than I had expected and wore a full beard. Not bad-looking, he was a very masculine type."

Maybe too masculine. Despite his progressive attitude about sex-change treatments, Dillon "appeared to have a very low opinion of women." It was an attitude that Cowell couldn't abide.[1] After they'd eaten, she lingered at the table to debate the issue of women's intelligence. They ordered coffee. Dillon gestured with his pipe as he lectured her about the differences between the male and female brain. He clearly liked to throw his opinions around, especially with a lady present.

Cowell played along. After all, if she was ever to emerge from the awful limbo of her body, she would need his help. Dillon seemed to relish his role as her protector, fingering his droll little beard, dropping Latin words and medical terms. He assured her that sex changes did exist. It was now possible for surgeons to entirely reshape the human body, he claimed. In fact, he possessed startling proof of exactly what medical science could do.

Then, Michael Dillon fell silent. He puffed smoke and fidgeted with his coffee cup but did not drink. He glanced up at Roberta, then, finally, spoke. "I don't really see why I shouldn't tell you. Five years ago I was a woman."[2]

More than a decade earlier, an athletic blonde named Laura Dillon roared through the streets of Bristol on her motorbike. She wore her hair short, and a sports jacket hid her breasts; a skirt, her only concession to femininity, flapped around her calves. With her broad shoulders, patrician accent, and Eton haircut, she could easily pass for a pampered young man. In fact, Laura had grown up thinking of herself as above the common lot. Her brother, the eighth baronet of Lismullen, presided over a threadbare estate in Ireland, and her family still retained a residue of an ancient fortune.

At first glance, Laura seemed to be a fellow just out of Oxford, dismounting his motorbike with a dashing leap. But blink again and Laura was nothing but a cross-dressed girl. People who passed her on the street couldn't help staring, confused by the double image she presented. The children and old ladies were the cruelest, shouting insults or demanding Laura explain herself. When they came toward her, Laura froze her face into a mask. She refused to let them see how they got to her.

Still, she preferred their taunts to the alternative: female clothing. Evening gowns terrified her—they invited young men to slide their arms around her waist. Ordinary dresses filled her with the sickening sense that she had been obliterated. She knew herself to be a man, a man who was disappearing inside a ridiculous body, underneath breasts and hips. She didn't think she could go on this way anymore.

Pills saved her. Laura Dillon had managed to get hold of testosterone pills in 1938, soon after she'd graduated from college. She became the first woman on record to take the drug with the intention of changing her sex. Over several years, the hormone therapy transformed her into a muscular, deep-voiced man with fuzz on his cheeks. As soon as Dillon could look entirely male, he became invisible. Pumping petrol at the garage where he worked, greasy in his coveralls, Dillon easily passed as just another workingman. More than passed. He became bland-looking, unremarkable, ordinary— which was what he'd always wanted. He could stroll down the street now, could step into a hardware store or a men's bathroom, without attracting the least bit of attention. By the early 1940s, Dillon had mustered the courage to leave the garage for medical school—under his male name.

But hormones could only take Dillon so far. If other men caught a glimpse of him in the locker room or public baths, they would immediately know he had been born female. So in the early 1940s, Dillon sought out Sir Harold Gillies, Britain's top plastic surgeon. Gillies had reconstructed the genitals of soldiers who'd been bombed or burned, but he had never built a penis from scratch on a woman's body. It would be grueling, and Gillies could not guarantee the results.

At least the operation would be legal. While an arcane law protected male genitals from "mutilation," no such bans applied to female genitals and reproductive organs.

Dillon would eventually undergo a series of thirteen operations to construct a penis.* He began the treatments in 1946, while he was a student at Trinity College medical school in Dublin, and he finished his surgeries in 1949, a year before he met Roberta Cowell. Gillies had to harvest skin for the new organ from Dillon's legs and stomach; Dillon suffered from oozing infections where the skin had been flayed; at times, he was so debilitated he had to walk with a cane.

And why did Dillon want the penis so badly? Not necessarily for sex. Rather, a penis would serve as a membership card into the world of men, their bathrooms, their rowing teams, and their gentlemen's clubs in London. The lack of a penis had held him back, "for without some form of external organ he could hardly undress for the shower with the rest of the crew,"[3] as Gillies noted. Furthermore, if Dillon fell ill, a penis would allow him to check into a hospital without having to explain why his genitals did not match the

---

*According to Dillon, the number of operations was thirteen and treatment ended in 1949. Gillies's medical notes contradict this recollection. According to Gillies, Dillon underwent seventeen operations, from 1946 through 1955, all of them presumably related to the creation and maintenance of the penis. I have chosen to hew to Dillon's recollection of events.

Sir Harold Gillies greets patients at Rooksdown in 1941. They were mangled by war, factory accidents, and cancer, but in the hospital they formed a close-knit community. *British Association of Plastic Surgeons*

rest of his body. A penis, along with the beard and the pipe, would hide his history, keep his secret that much safer. Dillon feared, above all, the tabloids. If the rumor got out that Michael Dillon, brother to a baronet, had once been a girl, the gossip would surely be trumpeted in every low-class newspaper in Britain. As Dillon saw it, a penis would help to safeguard his privacy and his family's honor.

So during the mid-1940s, Dillon lived a curious double life: he was both a medical student in Dublin and a patient in England. During the university term, he shadowed doctors on their hospital rounds, assisted in the surgical theater, and even performed an appendectomy. When the term ended, Dillon would ride a train through the English countryside to a small town called Basingstoke, home to Rooksdown House, the hospital overseen by Sir Harold Gillies. Here, men in military uniforms—their heads swaddled in bandages—lolled on park benches, putting cigarettes to the holes where their mouths should have been. Burn victims, a platoon of shot-up soldiers, children with cleft palates and survivors of factory accidents—Dillon joined this small society of the mutilated and maimed.

Sir Harold, as the patients called him, understood that recovery had as much to do with the mind as the body. Some of the patients at Rooksdown were so disfigured that, even with the best care, they would remain outcasts for the rest of their lives. Such patients had to be encouraged to relearn the art of happiness, which is why Sir Harold banished many of the rules that make hospitals such grim places and coaxed his charges into dancing the fox-trot, growing zinnias in the garden, or venturing out into the town surrounding the hospital for a beer. As a result, Rooksdown became the kind of place where, even in the middle of the night, you might come across a one-eyed man teaching himself to ride a bicycle down the hall. Or a burn victim wearing blue toenail polish. Or a surgeon pouring a pint of human blood into the tomato patch. "This was no ordinary place," Sir Harold wrote, with typical understatement.[4]

Dillon thrived at Rooksdown. He befriended a man with plastic ears, the girl who'd been scalped by a factory machine, and the navy officer who'd had his genitals ripped off by the gears of a machine. Stunted by years of ridicule, Dillon flowered in the tolerant atmosphere of Rooksdown: he turned witty, expansive, even popular. Dillon regarded the hospital as a year-round summer camp for misfits, and eagerly looked forward to seeing old friends every time he returned. One Christmas Eve, he made a grand entrance to a Rooksdown party in his wheelchair, and held court from its low-slung seat.

In the town surrounding the hospital, local people had grown used to seeing patients without noses or jaws walking around town. At the post office or on the street, Dillon and his friends could expect smiles and hallos from the villagers. But the patients knew that once they boarded the train, they would become pariahs at the very next town—passengers would flinch, stare, scuttle away from them.

Dillon had one advantage over most of the other patients: in that world beyond Basingstoke, he could pass as an ordinary man as long as he kept his clothes on. Still, this passing came at an emotional cost; a rigidly moral man, he had to lie constantly. When he returned to Dublin and ran into his fellow medical students, he had to invent stories to explain why he limped and sometimes had to walk with a cane. He blamed his troubles on the war—insinuating he'd been maimed in the Blitz, which he had not.

To keep the other students from asking questions, he cultivated a reputation as a stodgy bachelor, an older student who sequestered himself in the little house he owned. Now and then he asked young women out to dances and swooped around the floor in his white tie and tails. But Dillon didn't go on second dates. "One must not lead a girl on if one could not give her children. That was the basis of my ethics," he wrote later.[5]

Ethics weren't the half of it. How many women would be willing to risk the scandal of marrying the first artificial male? None, probably. At any rate, he didn't care to risk finding out. To marry a young woman, he would have to confess too much to her: the thirteen operations, the testosterone pills, the years of living as Laura. He was terrified, too, of what would happen if he ever did work up the nerve to tell a girlfriend about himself; he imagined how the smile would freeze on her face and her eyes would dart away, and how, when she looked back at him, she would no longer see him as a real man. He couldn't bear that. And so he avoided women. He brooded over the unfairness of his fate—it seemed he'd been given manhood, only to be denied a wife and children.

Still, he loved the way he looked in his tie and tails; he enjoyed a night of dancing, and an evening of playful flirting eased his loneliness a bit. So he took out a nurse or female student now and then, but he never let her closer than the arm's length of a waltz. He kept his distance by treating women in a "rough brotherly fashion," developing a reputation as a bit of a woman-hater. He liked to lecture his dates about how the female brain was more suited to housework than intellectual pursuits—a strategy guaranteed to stifle any romance.

Dillon claims that his misogyny was all an act, one of the tools he used to keep women from falling in love with him. But, in fact, he did believe the female mind to be a strange and rather frightening organ. Women had hurt him, over and over, even before the sex change. In Laura Dillon's teenage and university years, she had fallen in love with at least two straight women. Both of them had pushed Laura away. The worst part was that these would-be sweethearts had regarded her as a lesbian rather than as the man she wanted to be. Dillon had enjoyed only a few close friendships, and these had almost always been with men—backslapping boys who accepted Dillon as a brother.

So, women could not be trusted. Dillon had learned this early on. By age thirty-five, he had vowed never to fall in love.

And then Roberta Cowell slid into the seat across from him at that London restaurant, and he dared to hope again. Her wrists—slim and delicate from the estrogen treatments—peeped out of the cuffs of her sleeves. Her cheeks flamed pink, so soft below the short man's haircut. In the blur of Roberta Cowell's face, he could see the lovely ingénue she would become. Somewhere in there lived the one woman who could understand him, the one woman who could recognize him as a real man.

He had decided, from the logic of his profound isolation, that Cowell must be his soul mate. Dillon was lonely in the way we can all recognize, and he also suffered from a brand-new, twentieth-century solitude, too, one that had never existed before—the loneliness of a medical miracle, of the person who has experienced unique states of mind and body. He'd dared to confide in so few friends, and even the kindest of them had never really understood.

But now, he shared a table with the first person he'd ever met who'd entered that blur of hormones, who planned to transform her body just as he had. She relied on him, he liked to believe, not just as a doctor but also a man with a superior mind, who could guide her through difficulties. Dillon, too, had endured the torment of the in-between period when the hormones began pushing his body toward androgyny; he knew what it was like to stumble through a city street where passersby stared at him.

She was three years younger than he was, but seemed younger than that. She implored him for help; she needed him utterly. Dillon had waited his whole life for a woman to fasten her eyes on him the way she did, to ask for his protection.

And so he trusted Roberta immediately. By the end of lunch, he'd poured out his story to her—surprising even himself with his openness.

Then they parted. He returned to Dublin, where he was finishing up the last year of medical school, but Roberta continued to haunt him, to tug at his heart. He mailed her letters brimming with advice and tender confessions. "The chief feeling you arouse in me, Bobbie, is a desire to protect you and to treat you gently and steer you along," he wrote.[6] Whenever Dillon traveled to London, he made sure to call on her.

At one of these early meetings, "he . . . whipped out the penis, which he was very proud of," wrote Cowell. "It wasn't any kind of seduction scene. He just wanted me to see what medical science had achieved. I had never seen anything like it. It was huge, and in a constant state of semi-erection." She made a joke about the thing being rough-hewn. He didn't laugh. "Dillon did not exactly have the most perfectly developed sense of humor," according to Cowell.[7] Though, really, how could he have laughed? He'd unzipped for her; he'd showed her the evidence of his excruciating pain, all those operations and infections. He'd wanted her to see how he'd turned that suffering into a handsome piece of flesh. And all she could do was snigger.

Still, he refused to be discouraged. In his terrible loneliness, Roberta Cowell began to haunt his thoughts. For the first time in his life, Dillon allowed himself to believe that one person might be able to understand him. He sent her long confessional letters about his girlhood and his years at Oxford. He wanted her to know everything. She wrote back to him, when she could find the time. They talked on the phone, when she was in.

It was 1951 now; Cowell had turned herself into a va-va-voom peroxide blonde; she'd begun venturing out onto the streets of London in a wig, skirt, makeup. She had yet to go through the vaginal-construction surgery and the face-lift, but already she scorched the eyes of sailors as she flitted past them on the sidewalk.

Dillon was a virgin. He locked himself in his flat, stared at her photograph, and trembled with passion. And for the first time, he submitted to the feeling entirely. "I need to have two whiskies in me before I could start off 'my beloved Bobbie,'" he wrote her. "I have never called anyone that before and you know what my inhibitions are like."[8] In an effusion of letters, written on scraps of paper in between his rounds at the hospital where he worked as a student doctor, he poured out his feelings. She replied with brief notes, signed with nothing more than a scrawny "B." Dillon chalked that up to her female modesty. Sometimes he sent two letters a day. "Oh Bobbie, Oh Bobb-bee, come to me soon, I am wanting you all the time," he wrote to her. And: "You probably have had experience in the 'zones of eroticism' and I have had none. Still, you could teach me."[9] He wrote and wrote and wrote.

Roberta Cowell's side of the correspondence has not survived. Michael Dillon might have been a man given to impulsive leaps and grand gestures, but he was not delusional. He took it for granted that they would marry, and so she must have given him some reason for hope, some endearments on which to hook his passion.

Besides, as Dillon saw it, he was the only man she *could* marry. Once she had gone through her final surgery, they would be the only postoperative transsexuals in all of Britain. Surely they were fated to be together. Separately, they were two people who each guarded a secret, each of whom could be destroyed by a rumor or a tenacious reporter. Together, married, they would be much safer, much less likely to be exposed by the press; they would become blessedly invisible; just another frowsy heterosexual couple. That was Michael Dillon's ambition: to be ordinary. To melt into the crowd.

He wrote to tell her that as soon as he passed his examinations and became a doctor, they could go ahead and marry. He suggested a wedding at sea to avoid embarrassing their families. They might adopt children. They would certainly buy a proper set of china. If Dillon was aware that Cowell had already been married—to a woman—and fathered two daughters, he did not allow this to spoil his plans. Nor did he dwell too much on the other peculiarities of Cowell's past: as a man, Cowell had raced sports cars professionally and designed engines; she still liked to jump behind the wheel of a dragster and tear around the track. Surely, as a full-fledged woman, she'd give all that up to be a housewife?

Of course, she had reason to be demure about his offer; she was gathering the legal documents she would need to change from male to female; she was learning how to sway across the room and dangle her fork in a ladylike fashion. She would need time to adjust, he understood that.

His most pressing worry was his medical exams, which he thought he might fail. He felt he should have a job as a doctor—or the promise of one—before he asked Bobbie to marry him. He wrapped up a ring and nestled it inside an empty Players' cigarette package and sent it off to her, instructing her to tuck this gift away in a drawer. She was not to open it, not even to peek, until he'd passed his exams.

It was now the summer of 1951. Robert Cowell had become Roberta Cowell in the eyes of the British government. She had become a legal woman; Dillon was a legal man; they could marry, if they chose to. Dillon was cramming for his medical school finals. He thought he would probably fail the first time he took them—after all, he'd missed a lot of school for his trips to Rooksdown. He wore his lucky Oxford tie on the day of the final examination. The tie did its work: Dillon passed. He had become, to his own astonishment, a licensed doctor.

He fired off a letter to Bobbie. You can open the package now, he told her. Surely, she would take him seriously when she saw the diamond winking up at her from the palm of her hand. Didn't every woman want a diamond? He was a doctor now. Didn't every woman want that, too? He desperately needed a yes from her.

He had mailed the letter, and now he began the long, awful vigil, waiting for her reply. Dillon believed that if he and Bobbie threw their lot in together, they could live as other people from good families did: a housekeeper, a little garden, some handsome furniture. Roberta Cowell would make an excellent match. Like Dillon, she came from the upper classes; her father, Sir Ernest Cowell, had been the honorary surgeon to King George VI. If Dillon married and raised some adopted children, if he managed to shake off his reputation as a loner, he could do more than just pass as a born male. He would feel like one, too.

Like so many other people in the 1950s, Dillon had enormous hopes for the institution of marriage. It would be the badge of his citizenship, a passport into the land of the ordinary.

But would she have him? Would she agree to recognize the penis Gillies had made—that organ that had once inspired her hoots of laughter—as a penis indeed?

Several years before, in his book *Self*, Dillon had argued that transsexuals were ordinary people who just happened to be trapped in the wrong body. With the right surgeries and pills, he insisted, these people could become model citizens. It was a blazingly original idea in a time when most of the top medical minds still had no idea that transsexuals existed.

In *Self*, Dillon became one of the first scholars in the world to work out a classification system for gender identity and sexual desire. He insisted that homosexuals who cross-dressed (for instance, butch lesbians) belonged in a completely different category from transsexuals.* A butch lesbian might be able to hide out in a dress when she had to, to masquerade as a feminine woman in order to survive. But for a woman who knew herself to be a man, no such option existed; she *had* to stride down the street with a male swagger, *had* to wear a blazer. Transsexuals, he wrote, "have the most difficult life of all, for they cannot conceal their forms from curious eyes . . . Their peculiarities are forever being forced upon them by the thoughtless persons who gaze after them and loudly voice the question, 'Is that a man or a girl?' "[10] Homosexuals, at least, had the closet. Transsexuals did not. They were always on display.

Therefore, Dillon argued, the transsexual patient needed "his body [to] be made to fit his mind"; this was the only therapeutic model that would work for him. Transsexuals could not be talked out of their urges; psychiatry would not help. It was their bodies that didn't fit, and so the only cure was to give the patient a new body.[11]

Two decades later, Dr. Harry Benjamin would say much the same thing—only he would say it in much clearer language to a far broader audience. Benjamin, lifted to prominence by his famous friend Christine Jorgensen, became known as *the* expert on transsexuality in the 1950s—indeed, he is often credited with coining the term *transsexual* even though others had used the word before him. When Benjamin died at the age of 101, the *New York Times* described him as the "first student of transsexualism to discern that it was different from homosexuality or transvestism—phenomena with

---

*Dillon did not use the term *transsexual* in *Self*—the term had yet to enter common usage. Instead, he tended to use vague phrases (such as "these people") to indicate those who wished to change their sex.

which it was often confused. He also saw that transsexuals required medical assistance."[12]

In fact, the credit for these insights should properly go to Michael Dillon, who stumbled toward the same revelations during the early 1940s. Though Dillon was the first, he was never recognized as such. His obscure book, *Self*, reached only a small readership. At the time Dillon wrote, no surgeon in England or the United States would admit to performing a sex-change operation. Both countries had laws (the so-called mayhem statute) that forbid anyone from mutilating a man who could be drafted as a soldier—so physicians refused to amputate healthy testicles lest they be hauled into court. Laws aside, doctors were leery of operating on bodies to fix what they viewed to be a psychological condition, a mere neurosis. They'd sworn, under the Hippocratic oath, to do no harm. Harm, back then, included sex-change operations.

Dillon argued for a new kind of medical morality, one that took into account the patient's deepest urges. He'd met men at Rooksdown who'd had their faces burned into a red mask during war. These men would never have sweethearts or jobs unless their faces could be fixed. Transsexuals confronted the same situation; they felt stuck in deformed bodies that humiliated them. He insisted that the sex-change operation was not a violation of the Hippocratic oath—instead, it was a necessary treatment for people who needed to have their misshapen body restored to wholeness. Dillon had argued that if transsexuals were given the right body their troubles would end; he set out to prove this point with his own life. In 1950, he—and his surgeon, Gillies—believed he would settle down, sober up, marry, and muddle on as an ordinary man.

Of course, it's a hard job for anyone to act ordinary for years on end. The trouble for Dillon was he couldn't seem to stop editing his identity. When the sex change was behind him and his body sculpted to his satisfaction, Dillon decided to modify his mind. He pored over the books written by mystics in an attempt to calm his whirling thoughts and refurbish his personality. When books didn't save him, he pursued extreme treatments. Dillon wanted to re-shape his psyche as spectacularly as Sir Harold Gillies had once overhauled his body. His longing pulled him to India, years before hippies began beating a path there, in search of some final transformation. "The conquest of the body proved relatively easy," he observed at the end of his life. "But the conquest of the mind is a never-ending struggle."[13]

Dillon's tale proves just how far a human being can bend, how protean we are, how raw with possibility. He inhabited a dizzying array of roles: schoolgirl, doctor, besotted suitor, sailor, mystic. And yet, no matter how much he managed to mold his body and mind, Dillon could never manage to blot out a certain stubborn nub of himself, an essential quirk of his personality. Dillon could never change his desire for change.

CHAPTER 2
WHEN THERE'S NO WORD FOR IT

LAURA DILLON'S MOTHER DIED OF SEPSIS when Laura was ten days old. In 1915, a father could not be expected to look after small children alone, so Robert Dillon handed off his infant daughter and her fifteen-month-old brother to relatives; then he went on with the drinking binge that would eventually kill him. The children would be raised by their aunts in Folkestone, a seaside town set on cliffs over the English Channel, the kind of place that people say is perfect for children.

The aunts, middle-aged and frightened of youngsters, did their best to impersonate parents. When Bobby, Laura's older brother, turned eight, the aunts had him fitted him for his first suit and sent him off to an expensive boarding school. Laura, being the girl, attended a nearby day school and spent the rest of her hours cloistered in dark rooms. The aunts were determined to raise her to become a spinster like themselves, a lady always poised on the perch of ill health who dedicated her life to offending no one.

Aunt Toto suffered from a litany of ailments—headaches and anxiety—that ruled the house. She was tyrannical in the way only a delicate nineteenth-century-born lady could be, twisting Laura in the doily threads of guilt and pity. "You don't love me," she pleaded when Laura tried to leave the house. Toto's fears hemmed in the girl at every turn: Toto forbid her niece from going on camping trips with the Girl Guides (too expensive) or joining a field hockey team (too dangerous) or even bringing schoolmates home (they wouldn't want to come, dear).

Aunt Daisy, meanwhile, was useless. She floated in a world of her own, pretending not to hear what Toto said. Laura knew better than to hope that Aunt Daisy would offer her any kind of protection from their mutual tormentor.

In Toto's own time, she was regarded as a harmless eccentric; nowadays, she would no doubt be labeled an obsessive-compulsive hypochondriac with serious control issues. "Her affection was of the possessive type and she hated my making any close friends," Dillon wrote later. When Laura asked to go to tea at another girl's house, Toto forbid it. You're only bothering them, dear, Aunt Toto would say. She forbid Laura from accepting invitations and instructed her that she should not pester people by saying hello to them on the street. As a result, the girl became known around town as a sullen loner.

Laura's father was no help in protecting her from Toto. Occasionally, Daddy would whisk her brother, Bobby, to his flat in London or off to some lovely holiday. But he'd seldom take Laura along. Her birth had contributed to her mother's death, a crime that Daddy never seemed to forget. He abandoned Laura to the aunts, even at Christmas and Easter. She would be left alone to play in rooms crowded with antiques she was not allowed to touch, the clocks ticktocking out the endless hours of her brother's absence.

When her father died—Laura was nine years old—she perched in a church pew, gazing at the waxen doll in the coffin. She felt nothing. Beside her, Bobby wailed with grief. He'd adored Daddy; she'd hardly known the man.

Many years later, Dillon could summon up only three memories of his father, like three treasured snapshots: Daddy in his London flat, sitting up in his dressing gown, sick with hangover; Daddy leading Laura through the Regent Park Zoo; Daddy at the furniture store, pretending to haggle over a sixpence to tease the salesman. And that was all.

Back then, when she was just a little girl, her body belonged to her; her breasts had been nothing but dollops on her lean chest; the arms were wiry and strong. She shot at targets with her bow and arrow; built bookcases, a nail between her pursed lips; and beat up the occasional neighbor boy who deserved it. She read Tarzan books, dreamed of Africa, hopped along the rocks at the seashore, stared out at the distant, invisible lands where she would make her future.

Then, when she turned fifteen, the breasts bloated on her chest. They developed pernicious plans of their own, womanly plans that humiliated her, that made her terrified about what her body might decide to do next. She obliterated the breasts by flattening them under a belt—until one of the girls at her school told Laura she'd get

Laura Dillon as a teenager, posing seaside in Folkestone. *From the collection of Liz Hodgkinson*

cancer that way. So she unhooked the belt and tried to make peace with her breasts.

That year, she was gripped by a spiritual hunger. She wanted to find at least one solid thing—one truth—she could hold on to while her body metamorphosed. She plowed through books on theology and philosophy, hunting for answers, but no answers came. She puzzled over the habits of the aunts. What, ultimately, did their lives add up to? She could not say; their routines seemed pointless. What would constitute a meaningful life? She burned to know. It was as if Laura's two compulsions, to be male and to feel certain about some truth, awakened in her at the same time.

One day when she was seventeen or eighteen, she was scrambling up a path along a sea cliff alongside a boy about her age. When the two teenagers came to a gate, the boy swung it open and waited, gallantly, for Laura to proceed through first. It was the first time a boy had ever opened a door for her. "Suddenly, I was struck with an awful thought . . . : 'He thinks I'm a woman.' It was a horrible moment and I felt stunned," Dillon wrote later. "I had never thought of myself as [female] despite being technically a girl. I finished the walk in silence, the silence of despair, and he never knew what he had done to upset me. But life would never be the same again. People thought I was a woman. But I wasn't. I was just me."[1]

For all of us—transsexual and not—being misperceived, wrongly identified, or erased is one of the most terrible things that can happen. This seems to be particularly true when it comes to gender. To be taken for the wrong sex is to be blotted out, to be mis-seen in the most vital way. Worse, perhaps, is the nightmarish sense of not fitting together, of your insides not matching your outsides.

"Imagine . . . you feel great about yourself, . . . but when you look down, your body is the opposite sex from who you know yourself to be," writes activist Jamison Green. "Imagine what it would feel like to live with that discrepancy. That's something like what many transgendered people feel, what they have to deal with every day."[2]

Laura Dillon felt that. And, to compound her suffering, she did not have the word to describe her agony. She struggled, curled up in bed at night, to understand why she'd felt such dread when the gate had yawned open for her. It was 1932, and the word *transsexual* had not yet come into use. Even the most sophisticated doctors in Britain would not have been able to diagnose her.

It is a measure of her awkwardness that in her teenage years she managed to make only one close friend, and he was not only a middle-aged man but also the town vicar. This friendship, unlikely as it was, saved Laura. The vicar bought her the hockey stick that Toto refused to pay for, let her walk his family's dog because she was not allowed a pet of her own, and insisted, when the time came, that Laura must go to Oxford just as he had done.

In Laura's final years of high school, Toto had tried to convince her to drop out altogether; Toto had her own plans for Laura's future. The girl would accompany her aunt to the market every day, carrying the basket over one arm. That is, Laura would apprentice herself to become a spinster, would devote herself to serving her aunts in their old age, would spend the rest of her life in the twilight of that grim house in Folkestone.

But the vicar, along with a few other concerned adults in the town, had decided Laura was too spirited to survive as Toto's servant. She should go to university. That plan seemed especially feasible because she had a small inheritance, left to her by her father. The money would be enough to cover most of the tuition. Toto finally yielded.

The next fall, Laura Dillon boarded the train and watched the Folkestone station and her grim aunt Toto slip out of sight. A five-foot-six teenager with a wiry frame and a pile of blond hair, she was attractive enough to turn the heads of the men around her. That's why her aunt Toto had insisted that Laura ride in the ladies' carriage, a special train car that allowed only female passengers. Once the train was rolling, Laura jumped up and pushed her way into the aisle, already ignoring Aunt Toto's rules. She hurried into the car where the men sat, into the cigar smoke, the homburgs, and the wool suits. She found a seat and then watched as the whole world flickered past her window like frames in a film.

She was heading to Oxford—the very name thrilled her. The university had begun granting degrees to women only in 1920, and now strict quotas kept women in the minority at the university. Laura would be one of the lucky few. Soon enough, she was tramping across a university quad, the lilac shadow of an elm sliding over her face, a cache of philosophy books tucked under one arm. She had finally escaped Toto.

But she found that she had also brought certain other problems with her. Men opened doors for her all the time now; when they glanced at her, they saw nothing but a silly girl. The awful, unnamed despair—the mood that had first gripped her as she'd passed through that gate by the sea cliff—tormented her more and more often. She tried to avoid whatever brought it on, and as she did so, her life constricted. "For me, naturally, the social world was closed. I had long been finding it more and more difficult to . . . go to a party where young men were politely condescending," Dillon wrote.[3] Which in the 1930s ruled out just about every social function.

However, in the Oxford boathouse, she discovered a haven. The river sloshed against the pilings of the dock. A team of eight glided by, the cox yelling, "Stroke . . . stroke . . . stroke." Her despair lifted like the mist off the river. Her mind, often so muddled when she was on dry land, turned sharp. She discovered herself to be an enormously competent rower. In the water, you became a set of arms, a coil of muscles, a strong back. Her wiry body was made for the oar, for curling up and then the heaving backward thrust. By her second year at Oxford, she'd won a Blue—a sort of most-valuable-player award—and been elected president of the Oxford University

Woman's Boat Club. Outside the boathouse, however, she had no friends.

The Oxford men's team was famous around the country; when Oxford raced against Cambridge, newspapermen would stand along the banks snapping photographs, and mobs of fans would run alongside the boats, screaming encouragement. But the women's team—the one that Dillon captained—was a joke. At the time, it was an accepted medical truth that women must not overexert themselves, lest they injure their wombs and make themselves unfit for motherhood. So, wearing flowered skirts and bloomers, the women rowed downstream rather than up. Laura lobbied the college authorities to let the women compete like men: all in a pack, upstream, wearing uniforms. And uniforms, to Laura, meant blazers, shorts, and flannel trousers: men's clothing. It was the uniforms about which she became most passionate. She convinced a local sporting-goods store to donate outfits to her team, and she argued to anyone who would listen that the proper clothes could provide a winning edge to any athlete. She would know. As a little girl, Laura had hungered to wear a sailor's jacket just like her brother's, with brass buttons and braid anchors; she'd pleaded so relentlessly that the aunts had finally let her have one, and she'd worn it with a pillbox sailor's cap that read H.M.S. RENOWN. That suit had stood for the very essence of what she wanted—some fluttering vision of her future self.

Now, she'd invented a grown-up version of that sailor's suit. And, even more thrillingly, she commanded a group of women dressed in similar attire. She had managed to make a small corner of the world conform to her vision of how things should be. On the river near the Oxford boathouse, women pumped at the oars, straining with masculine abandon, in their handsome blazers and caps. Decades later, typing his life story in India, Michael Dillon could still recall exactly what the rowing uniform had looked like: the blue piping on the white vest, the crossed-oars insignia on the schoolboy cap, the blazer, and the snappy flannel trousers.

For the first time in her life, Laura had found a place where she was allowed to dress and act exactly as she pleased. But this little society that Laura had invented proved to be fragile indeed.

One day, she was launching a boat on the stretch of river usually reserved for the male rowers. A newspaper photographer was hanging around just then, snapping pictures to promote the upcoming match between the Oxford and Cambridge men's teams. Laura was stepping into the boat—her schoolboy haircut hidden under the cap, her blazer turning her figure boxy—when the photographer aimed his camera at her. She hardly noticed.

The next day, the *Daily Mirror*—a tabloid newspaper that in those days reported on mind-reading dogs, sex perverts, and haunted houses—included her in its freak show. A photo depicted "L. M. Dillon" as a bizarre, androgynous person caught in the glare of a flashbulb. Underneath the picture, a caption demanded to know what the creature was: "Man or woman?"

She was not even sure how to answer that question herself, and now people all over England would flip through the newspaper and ask themselves, "Who's this 'L. M. Dillon?' " Including the aunts.

Years before, Laura's brother, Bobby, had become a member of the landed gentry. He was ten years old at the time. The children's uncle and their father had died within three weeks of one another, leaving Bobby as the next male heir to a title that dated back centuries: baronet of Lismullen. It was an honor without many perks. The tiny estate attached to Bobby's title was located in county Meath, Ireland, a hotbed of resistance to British rule. Indeed, Bobby inherited a manor house that was nothing but a pile of charred wood. It had been destroyed by Sinn Féin some years before. Still, the aunts—and Bobby himself—looked on the title of baronet as an honor that elevated the entire family, one that they must all live up to.

And now Laura had smeared the family name through the grime

of newsprint. The aunts wrote her furious letters, accusing her of making herself into a freak. Bobby would hardly have anything to do with her. His sister—an inch taller, with muscle-bound arms—mocked him with her very appearance. Seeing them together, people would surely joke that she would have made a better baronet. It had always been that way. When they were little, the grown-ups noticed how Laura loved to play Indian and how Bobby preferred to tinkle the piano. She should have been the boy, they'd cluck. Now here was Laura in the tabloids, an Oxford rower of indeterminate gender.

After that unfortunate incident, the aunts expected that Laura would finally have learned her lesson. Surely, when she came home for summer vacation this time, she'd have prettied herself up in a dress. But, no. When Laura stepped off the train, she wore her own odd costume: a rowing blazer and a boy's haircut.

Laura simply could not change. "It may be asked why I needed to dress in 'mannish' way or have an Eton crop [hairstyle], thus calling attention to myself. It is impossible to explain to anyone who has not had the same experience," Dillon wrote later. "I could not do other than I did."[4] Wearing a dress threw her into anguish so excruciating that she compared it to the pain of having her teeth drilled. To be caught in anything frilly was to be humiliated. She wore as much men's clothing as she dared.

In November of 1928, the author Radclyffe Hall swept into a London courthouse decked out in a leather driving coat and a cowboy hat. Independently wealthy, she behaved exactly as she pleased, and what pleased her was to call herself John, strut around in the finest men's suits, and write a candid semiautobiographical novel called *The Well of Loneliness*, which shocked the British nation.

The novel tells the story of a girl born to landed gentry—only she is not exactly a girl. Her father understands that his infant daughter was meant to be a boy, and so he names her Stephen; as she grows up, he encourages her to fence and argue and ride astride a horse like a man. Though the novel offers nothing more explicitly homosexual than a kiss, its author was immediately hauled into court on obscenity charges. Hall's novel had acknowledged that women could desire each other sexually—and that was enough to make the book dangerous. In the 1920s, many British people simply had no idea that lesbians existed. Paradoxically, the highly publicized obscenity trial would put lesbianism on the front pages and help to nurture a new gay subculture.

The magistrate in the 1928 trial ruled that every copy of the novel would have to be destroyed; the book remained under a ban until 1949. But bootlegged copies circulated among a fast-growing underground; women secreted copies of it in paper bags and passed it around to one another. With almost no other such books available, *The Well of Loneliness* became the final word on female homosexuality. At Oxford, lesbians dressed like Stephen in lovely wool trousers and blazingly white button-down shirts; and Radclyffe Hall's haircut—the so-called Eton crop—became a fad. The hair would be clipped close to the skull all over, except for a curtain of bangs that fell across the forehead and threatened to fall into the nearest eye; the bangs could be tossed aside with a haughty rearing of the head. The haircut, named after the most exclusive boys' school in England, connoted not just maleness but also privilege—the freedom of women who'd inherited their wealth and would never have to marry.

The Well of Loneliness inspired a mannish style that would endure for decades—and that confused many gay women who had no urge to cross-dress. One lesbian, who encountered the book in 1949, felt that it was more harmful than helpful as she tried to sort out her own identity: "It . . . sold me the idea that all lesbians were masculine and tall and handsome and Stephenish."[5]

A number of modern scholars have echoed this point: the first and most famous "lesbian novel" might actually describe a woman who identified as a male—in today's lingo, Stephen would be called a transgendered man. But such was the invisibility of female-to-male transsexuals during the 1920s and 1930s that they were assumed to be lesbians.

This is exactly what happened to Laura. A sophisticated friend at Oxford had told Laura that she was a "homosexual." Laura had never heard the word before, but she resolved that if she was a homosexual, well then, fine, she would wear her diagnosis with dignity, like an ugly but serviceable suit. When she went home to Folkestone after the Oxford term ended, she thought she should tell *someone* in the family. She chose Aunt Edie as her confidante—a married sister of Toto and Daisy's who'd once been a tennis star. Laura biked over to her aunt Edie's house one afternoon, and after they'd sat down to tea, announced that she was a homosexual.

Aunt Edie burst out laughing. What have you been reading to put this nonsense into your head? You must get married right away to cure this silliness, Aunt Edie declared.

Laura biked away, pedaling in slow motion, shattered. She would get no help from her family.

No one seemed to understand her—not even the homosexuals. At Oxford, Laura ran into a friend from high school who'd grown into a confident lesbian. This friend urged Laura to stop being so repressed and "take a woman"—a piece of advice meant kindly but as unhelpful, in its way, as Aunt Edie's. "This advice was to be given to me again and again, even by well-known doctors, yet never did I take it. Somehow it seemed wrong," Dillon wrote.[6]

Laura did have eyes for women—but they always seemed to be straight women on the verge of marriage. She fell torridly in love with a Shirley Temple look-alike on her rowing team. When Laura confessed her passion, the girl rebuffed her as kindly as possible: if Laura had been a man, the girl said, she would no doubt have fallen in love. And then the adorable blonde went off and engaged herself to some suitor.

Laura could not seem to develop an enthusiasm for lesbian sex; she would have had to strip off her blazer and the bindings on her chest, until she was naked and female; her lover would have desired exactly what Laura hated about her body. Nor did she belong in Oxford's lesbian subculture, striding arm in arm across campus with the bluestockings, discussing women's right to work.

After many months of trying to be one, Laura began to realize that she wasn't a homosexual after all. She appeared to be something else, and she still knew no name for it.

Had she grown up in Berlin, she might have known. For there, during a brief flowering of sexual tolerance between the wars, doctors had begun to diagnose patients like her, had written hundreds of pages about cross-dressers and people who ached to switch sex; they had even begun to treat these people and advocate for their rights.

In 1919, Magnus Hirschfeld—a doctor, homosexual, and activist—founded the world's first center devoted to research of sexuality and gender, the Institute for Sexual Science in Berlin, a base from which he could launch the first large-scale studies of human sexuality. Decades before Alfred Kinsey, Hirschfeld used modern techniques to understand the varieties of human desire: he handed out questionnaires, interviewed hundreds of people, and observed behavior in nightclubs and bars.

Berlin in the teens and twenties teemed with spit-curled lesbians and rouged gentlemen in petticoats; in those first spangled decades of the twentieth century, Berlin had become the capital of cross-dressing. Hirschfeld mingled easily in working-class gay bars and at outré theater performances and at lavish costumes balls held in secret locations, where he presided as a guest of honor. It was only natural that he should begin to study the erotic power of clothing. In 1910, Hirschfeld authored the first observational study of people who cross-dress, naming them *transvestites*. Today, we use the word more narrowly than Hirschfeld did; currently, psychologists define a transvestite as a person (often heterosexual, usually male) who derives sexual pleasure from costume. Hirschfeld used the word more inclusively: a transvestite was anyone who dressed in drag for any reason, including people we would now call transsexual or transgendered—people who cross-dress to express their core identity. In 1923, he became the first author to use the term *transsexual* in a medical paper to describe a class of men and women who were gripped by the conviction that they'd been born into the wrong body.

At the Institute for Sexual Science, Hirschfeld amassed over twenty thousand scholarly books, files full of sexual memoirs, a museum of fetish art, samples of sperm and ovarian tissue, lab equipment, and surgeons to treat patients. Hirschfeld and his staff had collected, among other wonders, "sixty pairs of women's calf boots, some of which laced right up to the thigh," according to Ludwig Levy Lenz, a surgeon at the institute. "We had, too, boxes containing plaits and buns gleaned by a hair fetishist. We had a beautiful collection of the most luxurious and expensive women's underwear; we had masturbatory apparatus, ranging from the simple godmiche to an electrically operated stimulator. We had a big collection of unpublished poems dealing with love, of cover girls, cabaret posters, old Egyption Phalli."[7]

Hirschfeld became one of the foremost agitators against the Nazi Party and its punishment and ostracism of homosexuals. Nonetheless, he did not turn away Nazi Party members who came to the institute begging for help with their strange cravings. "Not ten percent of [the Nazis] were sexually normal," according to Lenz.[8] Party members wanted relief from sexual obsession, impotence, an urge to cross-dress, a craving to touch young boys. The medical histories of these Nazis accumulated in the back rooms of the institute, alongside the hairpieces and masturbatory machines. By the early 1930s, Hirschfeld held the secrets of a number of Hitler's followers.

"We knew too much," Lenz wrote, and if they stayed in Germany, they would surely be killed.[9] By 1933, when the Nazis came to power, Hirschfeld fled to Switzerland; Lenz hid out in Paris. In the spring of 1933, Hirschfeld learned that the institute had been razed to the ground by Nazi rioters.

"The government has dissolved our Institute, has taken by force the greatest part of our library and many other items, and willfully destroyed them," Hirschfeld wrote to friends from his haven in Switzerland. "Most of the books . . . were removed with violence, and four days later everything was thrown onto an auto-da-fé and burnt to cinders. Even the bronze of my head . . . was flung into the fire."[10]

And the world more or less forgot about Hirschfeld and his scientific advances. Even in 1932, that last year the institute stayed open—that year when Laura Dillon stared at an open gate and felt a nameless terror—few people outside of Berlin knew that a place had once existed where doctors systematically studied sex and clothing and erotic drawings in order to describe modes of human behavior. Laura Dillon certainly did not know about the institute. Nor would her older self, Michael Dillon, ever learn about Hirschfeld or read his book, *Die Transvestiten,* which included case studies of people who cross-dressed for all kinds of reasons; the book would not be translated into English until 1991, decades after Dillon was gone.

She did not have a word for what she was. She did not have a diagnosis. So she bought a pipe. She brought it back to her room, packed it with a wad of tobacco, lit it up, and took an experimental puff. She gagged and coughed. Her lungs burned. In secret, Laura taught herself to suck on a pipe as if she were an Oxford don, to puff thoughtfully and then to exhale the pungent smell of maleness. She was beginning to guess at the shape of her true self; she was starting to know what she'd need to survive.

At Oxford, men existed apart from her, beyond her reach. They moved in clumps through the quad, laughing at jokes she couldn't quite hear; they retreated behind heavy doors to rooms for gentlemen; they sauntered off to boxing matches at stadiums that did not allow ladies in. How could she become one of them? If she were to chum up to a man, he would surely take it the wrong way; he'd want to make love to her.

That's why she needed to smoke. If any man fell for her, she decided, she would show him the pipe, and that would explain everything. She couldn't say she was a "homosexual," because that was not true. For now, the pipe—that piece of wood carved into the shape of a question mark—would have to symbolize whatever she was.

And she had a new friend, which was as much a comfort as the pipe. Bill had come to Oxford on scholarship from the Midlands; his nasal accent marked him as a poor boy among the velvet-voweled, posh undergraduates. He was an outsider, too, and so Laura picked him to be the first best friend of her adult life. Over coffee one day, she blurted out that she wanted to live like a man. She'd been terrified that Bill might laugh at her, but instead he listened sympathetically. From that day on, he accepted Laura as a brother.

They shopped together for sport coats and flannel trousers; and he smuggled Laura into Oxford boxing matches. Now, dressed in drag, she had gained entrance to this sweat-reeking, smoky theater where all eyes focused on the two slick bodies in the ring, locked in an embrace, man-to-man. She felt, perhaps for the first time in her life, that she belonged.

During the holidays, when she traveled home to Folkestone, the aunts met her at the station, tut-tutting at her jacket and boy's haircut; so she took the train to Folkestone less and less. Oxford had become home. Within the wide arms of the Gothic buildings she could do pretty much as she pleased. Oxford, after all, was a university town, teeming with theatrical young men with rouge on their cheeks, with young women who scribbled manifestos in their notebooks. Laura did not draw much attention when she hurried to class in her schoolboy blazers. By her final year, she even dared to roar around town astride a motorcycle; she had bought a two-stroke Coventry-Eagle.

And she'd discovered that she was not the only one—she had met another female undergraduate who knew herself to be a man.* Laura and her friend declared themselves brothers and became an athletic duo: together, they rowed for miles in a racing boat built for two, a skittish shell that was only sixteen inches wide and so unsteady that it would tip all but the best athletes into the water. They were so close, they no longer needed words; instead they communicated through shift of weights and subtle twists of their oars in the water. They became sparring partners, too, taking boxing instructions from an old army man at the university, who found his female pupils amusing.

This "brother" of Laura's would be the only other woman she ever met who shared her desire to become a man. They spent entire days out on the river during the summer, communicating through the dip of an oar or a shift of weight, and then at night found hotels close to the shore and collapsed into exhausted sleep. They shared their hotel rooms chastely. They were, after all, brothers.

Still without a label for herself, Laura had at least begun to understand the nature of her compulsions. She wanted to stride down the street and be *seen* as a man, and not just any kind of man either: she was the sort who smoked a pipe, read classics in the original

---

*In his autobiographical manuscript, Dillon withheld the names of many of his friends—including this rowing partner at Oxford. After being hounded and exposed by the tabloids, he took pains to ensure that he would not inflict a similar humiliation on anyone mentioned in his book.

Greek, and made an excellent team captain. Laura Dillon was an Oxford man.

"Oxford! Even now, when I am supposed to have renounced the world and to have become detached from worldly pleasures, the thought of Oxford still has the power to move me," Michael Dillon wrote in the late 1950s. Dillon always treasured the way *Oxford* rolled off his tongue. It was a word like a golden key that would admit you into the world of men of the proper class, to rooms outfitted with leather and redolent with smoke and shaving cream. "If you mention the word 'Oxford' to an old Oxford man, wherever he may be in the world, at once a faraway look comes into his eyes," Dillon wrote.[11]

Oxford had been the first place where Laura belonged, the first place where, however conditionally, she had been able to live as a man. And then, in 1938, she graduated and had to start all over again, learning how to survive as a man in a woman's body in the outside world. Or, rather, she began to understand that such an existence would not be possible—that she was an impossible being.

After university, she found a job at a research laboratory in the countryside of Gloucestershire. She settled into a boardinghouse in a small village, lost in a maze of narrow cobblestoned streets. She did not make friends. Nights in the boardinghouse, she ate at a table loud with cockney chatter where the workingmen grabbed for the gravy boats and the bread platters. Their habits bewildered her. Had she been an ordinary young lady, she might have been married by now; or she would have moved to the Dillon estate in Ireland, where her brother, Bobby, had set himself up as a country squire; or she might have returned to Folkestone to become a teacher, dropping in on the aunts every Sunday for tea.

But Laura could no longer consider such a life. Her compulsion to cross-dress had grown stronger every year, and it was all she could do to keep herself from trousers. In Gloucestershire, she stomped around in a dowdy skirt, which she topped with a sport jacket, her short hair flopping over her forehead, so she appeared to be a sideshow exhibit, a half-man/half-woman with the dividing line at her waist. On buses and in restaurants, people would lean into each other and ask, "Is that a man or a girl?" They spoke loudly, caring nothing for her feelings, as if she were deaf or stupid; they wanted to see her flinch. When she spotted a pack of children coming toward her, she'd steel herself for their taunts. She learned how to suffer while keeping her face fixed in a mask of indifference. She refused to cringe.

But she loved her work. She'd landed a job at a laboratory where researchers dissected brains and studied samples that had been taken from living patients—the kind of "man's job" that had only become available to women because of the looming war. The doctors at the lab were polite enough to ignore the young woman's odd appearance, especially after she proved to be enormously competent.

She spent her days handling brains fresh from the skull, bloody and red as any piece of meat, and brains in vats of formaldehyde, gray and reeking. How could you locate the home of maleness or femaleness inside these hunks of gray matter? The question had become urgent for her. Outside the lab, she endured jeers and taunts because she could not present herself as either male or female; she had landed in what Radclyffe Hall named the "no man's land between the sexes," that loneliest place of all. Without a sex, she would not be treated as a human being. She would remain a "museum piece" (as Dillon put it later), gawked at like an exhibit in a cage. Perhaps by studying the brain and its links to the body she would learn what had gone wrong with her. She would learn how to be seen as a person again.

Or perhaps she would take the more dangerous route to social acceptance: the military. In Hall's novel, *The Well of Loneliness*, Stephen first earns social acceptance when she volunteers to drive ambulances into the battlefield during the Great War. Hall sketches portraits of gay men and lesbians, cross-dressers, and mannish middle-aged ladies who became heroes by risking their lives. Once seen as freaks, they emerged from the battlefields as human beings—after the sacrifices they'd made, their countrymen had to acknowledge their bravery. But Radclyffe Hall had been describing the situation in the darkest days of the Great War, when the British military would accept anyone—anyone at all.

It was still too early in *this* war for people like Laura. In 1939, she signed up with the Women's Auxiliary Air Force (WAAF) to deliver dispatches on her motorcycle, but the commander in charge fired her in a week—Laura was deemed too mannish to sleep in the women's dorm. Of course, she was not enough of a man yet to wear a navy uniform as her father had. She had fallen into that slushy canal between the sexes. Even the military wouldn't have her.

She'd been ejected from her family, shunned as an oddity, and left out of the marches and the patriotic parades. Now, she only saw one way to keep herself from going mad or dying of grief: she would have to find some way to become a man, really and truly. Laura began to fantasize that somewhere a doctor might know a secret, a magic formula, a fix. She had no reason to hope. As far as she knew, no one in the world had ever changed sex, and the doctors would be able to offer her nothing. But still, it seemed her only chance of a decent life.

When she learned that a clinician at the Bristol Royal Infirmary specialized in sex problems, she screwed up her courage and made an appointment. Laura had never before confided her suffering to any medical expert. But now she slung her leg over her motorbike and roared toward nearby Bristol, to find out whether medical science had anything to offer.

In 1939, Dr. George Foss sat across his desk from one of the strangest patients he'd ever seen. The creature, dressed in a rumpled mélange of male and female costume, wanted to live as a man or not at all. Foss was delighted. How fascinating! Who knew that such compulsions existed? Laura Dillon would make a perfect experimental subject.

For two years, Foss had been administering high doses of testosterone to women. The drug had just hit the market and no one knew much about it, which added to its mystique and helped to give doctors the idea that it could cure anything at all. It was rumored to be an elixir for men, treating every ill from impotence to the pains of old age. Foss hit on the idea that testosterone might work magic on women, too. He specialized in treating patients who had endured months of uninterrupted menstruation, women who'd dragged themselves into his office pale and exhausted and desperate for relief. In 1938, he published a study of the drug's effects on sixteen such patients: he found that massive doses of testosterone propionate (an injectable form of the drug) would stop some women from bleeding. Therefore, Foss touted the drug as a "valuable addition to gynecological practice." He acknowledged that the drug might have dangerous side effects, but insisted that he had not seen anything to worry him.[12] Of course, some women had noticed that the drug made their clitorises swell—but Foss considered that a plus. "I do not regard this [enlargement of the clitoris] as an unpleasant effect," he wrote.[13] Also, sometimes his patients' breasts shrank—but again, not necessarily a bad thing, Foss opined. And he did admit that one woman's voice had deepened after she'd begun treatment, so that she began speaking like a "gruff male." But he doubted whether this had anything to do with the testosterone.[14]

Now Miss Dillon sat on the other side of his desk from him, begging to be made into a man. What an opportunity! What an interesting experiment! Here was a female patient happy to test out much higher doses than the others would tolerate, a patient who *wanted* side effects. Miss Dillon's case might make a name for him. He could become the first researcher ever to find out what extremely high doses of testosterone could do to a woman's body—and her mind.

Miss Dillon, he told her, I can help you. He promised Laura that he would inject her with the one drug that offered her hope of becoming masculine. But before he began the experiment, she would have to meet with one of his colleagues, a psychiatrist, who would study her unusual desire to become a man.

Laura complied. She met with the psychiatrist and answered a battery of questions. Then she returned to Foss's office many days later, in a flutter of hopefulness.

She found her benefactor utterly changed. Nervous and evasive, he declared that the experiment was off and he would have nothing more to do with her. Most likely, a colleague had warned Foss away from performing such a risky stunt on a patient. Whatever the reason, Foss refused to help Laura, claiming that he expected to receive his military call-up papers and be shipped off to the front any day now.

Laura sputtered home on her motorbike, sunk in depression. Dr. Foss had been her one hope. Now, with the war on and doctors going overseas, it could be years before she found any help with her body.

It did not occur to her that she had the solution to her problems, and it lay as close as her own pocket, where a vial of pills rattled with every bump of the motorbike. At the end of her consultation with Foss, he had thrown the medication across his desk to her. He'd suggested she see what happened when she dosed herself, without telling her anything about the effect the drug might have.

CHAPTER 3
MAGIC PILLS

BEHIND THE LOCKED DOOR OF HER RENTED ROOM, Laura Dillon began experimenting on herself. She pressed a pill onto her tongue and swallowed. She examined herself in the mirror. At first, she saw nothing, no changes at all.

Indeed, for Laura, her dealings with Dr. Foss had only one immediate side effect: her deepest secret was no longer a secret. One day at the lab, she noticed that people were sniggering as she walked by. Some of them called out, "Miss Dillon wants to become a man!" One of the secretaries pulled Laura aside and told her what had happened: the psychiatrist she'd gone to see—Dr. Foss's colleague— had gossiped about her case at a dinner party. Laura's story had spread around town. Now everyone knew.

That was it for Laura. She packed and fled, ending up in Bristol— the nearby city. Immediately, she lost herself in the bustle of traffic, in the crush of people who would never know her. The spires of ships bobbed over the roofs of warehouses; factories drew armies of workers; and buses rumbled along the streets. In Bristol, she could vanish.

At a cavernous garage with a Help Wanted sign in its window, she presented herself to the boss, offering a driver's license for his inspection. The boss held it between a greasy thumb and forefinger as he squinted at the name and then at the strange-looking person before him. All right, Miss Dillon, he said, you're hired.

Of course she was. The young men of Bristol had vanished, summoned away by letters in the mail. Women flocked into the Bristol Aeroplane Factory to work on the line. Help Wanted signs beckoned from doorways and shop windows everywhere. A young woman with an Oxford education could have had her choice of jobs. Except that Laura was no longer a woman, exactly.

She'd become a person in between, liminal, nervous-making, freakish. The testosterone had started to deepen her voice and bulk her muscles. She did not know what would come next—whether the drug would leave her stuck in androgyny or whether it would make a man of her. In those early years, chemists and physicians still thought of testosterone as a tonic for old men, a rejuvenating elixir that would forestall aging, mental decline, and impotence. The pills had been designed for bald-headed codgers who wanted to get their spark back. It was not supposed to turn women into men.

At the beginning of the twentieth century, the ovaries and testicles were shrouded in mystery; they were secret islands in the body that scientists had only just begun to explore. No researcher had managed to isolate estrogen or testosterone, nor indeed did these substances have names. Scientists knew sex hormones existed only because of their effects: the horn of the bull, the milk of the cow, the peacock's fan, and the soprano's trembling high note. But no one had yet explained how the testicles and the ovaries managed to shape almost every other part of the animal, including its personality.

In the early twentieth century, a Viennese gynecologist named Josef Halban theorized that both the male and female sex organs released the same chemical into the bloodstream. After all, males and females produced identical substances in their thyroid glands; a ram, for instance, could receive a thyroid-gland transplant from an ewe and it would remain a ram. So, Halban believed, if a boy were to be castrated and have an ovary implanted into his body, he would still grow into a normal man. According to Halban, the substances released by the ovary did no more than kick-start puberty; it contained no special power to feminize the body.[1]

In 1912 and 1913, a Viennese colleague of Halban's, Eugen Steinach, proved him wrong with a set of studies that had something of the circus act in them. Steinach published results that suggested that the ovaries and testicles produced different chemicals, and that these excretions exerted their own unique effects on the body. He demonstrated his point by performing some of the world's first sex changes. On guinea pigs. Steinach castrated young animals, then transplanted ovaries into males and testicles into the females. The male guinea pigs grew to maturity bathed in female hormones; as a result, they did not develop into ordinary males. Far from it. Steinach's altered guinea pigs behaved shockingly like the other sex. Milk dribbled from the males' nipples, and they exuded "feminine sex appeal," according to Steinach, meaning they responded coyly to the advances of other males.[2] Meanwhile, the female guinea pigs' clitorises swelled into small penises; they grunted; they fought; they chased other females around the cages; they displayed all kinds of unladylike behavior. Steinach had proved, he believed, that "in every individual there is the . . . potential for either sex."[3] Therefore, he thought it was sex hormones, not some predetermined pattern in our bodies, that caused us to become male or female.

He vividly illustrated his point with a photograph of a male-born guinea pig suckling a couple of babies. The guinea pig's little eye glitters inscrutably as the creature stands on its tiptoes to let the two babies suck milk from its belly—a haunting and eerie testament to just how much power hormones might have to shape our personalities, our very selves.

Steinach had proved the power of sex hormones to blur the lines between male and female. But he had no interest in changing men into women or vice versa. Instead, he dreamed of rejuvenation. If he could find a way to deliver testicle juices into the bodies of old men, initiating a second puberty, octogenarians would throw away their canes and perform feats of strength! His guinea pig sex-change operations were only the way station on the road to a different destination. Steinach was determined to defeat death itself.

And this made him famous. Though he's largely forgotten now, Steinach was so well known in the 1920s that his name became a verb. A man "got Steinached" by submitting to a fifteen-minute operation that was supposed to stimulate his testicles to produce more of the hormones that masculinized the body. (Words such as *testosterone* and *androgen* and *steroid* had not yet come into common use, but Steinach grasped that the testes produced a chemical that bulked up muscle and amped up the sex drive, and whatever that as-yet-unnamed chemical was, he wanted to give men more of it.) Steinach's fifteen-minute rejuvenating operation was nothing more than a glorified vasectomy; he believed that by cutting or blocking the tubes that release sperm from the testes, he could raise levels of "vital juices" in the body. His operation was utterly wrongheaded. It did nothing to alter hormone levels, but it did apparently act as a powerful placebo. Men madly pursued the cure during the 1920s, and it became *the* fad operation of its era.

"For several years past, that great biologist, Dr. Steinach, Director of the Biological Institute in Vienna, had been much discussed in European scientific circles, owing to his successful experiments on rats and guinea pigs, which he had restored to youth and reproductivity," wrote bon vivant and novelist Gertrude Atherton. "He had then operated on men with equal success. I had heard of him myself, for a well-known Englishman of sixty-odd had been re-energized by Steinach, and was so enthusiastic that he announced he would take Albert Hall and tell the world about it. But alas, he felt so young and energetic that he plunged into the wild life of a young man about town, caught pneumonia, and died."[4] In fact, Steinach's patient Albert Wilson died the day before he could give his lecture,

"How I Was Made Twenty Years Younger." Even that turn of events failed to dampen enthusiasm for the Steinach operation.

W. B. Yeats got Steinached in 1934, in hopes of shaking off depression and satisfying his twenty-seven-year-old girlfriend; Yeats claimed that the operation had given him a surge of vigor that cured his writer's block. Even Sigmund Freud—the very model of a skeptical thinker—got Steinached, in 1926. Freud, worn down by his battle with cancer of the jaw, sought out the operation in secret. He confided in Harry Benjamin that the treatment had worked wonders; he brimmed with energy and his jaw seemed to be healing. Freud begged Benjamin to tell no one he'd resorted to the fad operation until after his death.[5]

In the 1920s—an era drunk on slim hips and jazz and hot-cha-cha, on bare legs and bathtub gin—growing old suddenly seemed unacceptable. Women bound their breasts in hopes of looking like fourteen-year-olds. F. Scott Fitzgerald declared that there were no second acts. Advertisements for creams and tonics promised pep, glamour, zip. In 1928, U.S. doctors met for the first national conference ever on the problems of old age—they dared to discuss what would have seemed unthinkable only a few decades ago: a "cure" for old age.[6]

Sex hormones—with their power to kick off puberty, to soften skin and build muscle—offered the most hope. Even today, researchers debate whether testosterone or estrogen should be taken to ameliorate the symptoms of old age. While the benefits remain unclear, we do know that hormone treatments come with significant risks, including prostate and breast cancer, heart disease and stroke.

In the 1920s, estrogen and testosterone had yet to be synthesized in large enough quantities to make them usable as drugs. Therefore, an entire field of quack medicine, called organology, bloomed. Its primary purpose: to change the levels of sex hormones in people's bodies in an era before drugs were available to do just that.

In 1923, a surgeon named Serge Voronoff snapped off the lights in a lecture room at the International Congress of Surgeons in London and showed a series of before-and-after movies of some of his patients: decrepit old men sprung out of sickbeds to row down a river. The surgeon claimed that he'd given the men their vigor by grafting slices of chimpanzee testicles into their gonads. The procedure was simple: Voronoff would etherize both man and chimp and place them side by side on operating tables. He would then cut slivers from the chimp's testicles and insert them into the man's testicles. For Voronoff, there was only one hitch: not enough chimps.[7]

In the United States, a doctor with a mail-order degree from the Kansas City Eclectic Medical University hawked his own cheapo version of the Voronoff treatment. Dr. John Brinkley used goats instead of chimpanzees—which drastically reduced the price of the operation. If you came into Brinkley's "hospital" in Kansas, you could get yourself rejuvenated for under a thousand dollars. Hell, you could even pick out your own goat.

"The subject for discussion at this time is your health. Not my health, but the health of my listeners and friends throughout radioland," Doc Brinkley would implore over the airwaves of KFKB, his own radio station. Old men flocked to Milford, Kansas, and as many as sixty a day left with slices of goats sewn into their testicles.

The monkey- and goat-gland practitioners, for all their promises, did not give their patients much beyond nasty infections. By the 1930s, they'd mostly packed up and scuttled away—driven off by the medical advances that made them obsolete. During that decade, lab-manufactured, synthetic testosterone and estrogen both became available. But even then, the dream of life extension died hard. For instance, in 1935, when Lavoslav Ruzicka and his partner Adolf Butenandt produced the first synthesized testosterone, most scientists still believed that it might provide the key to recapturing youth. "The male hormone has been isolated from the testes," Ruzicka told the *New York Times* that year. "We may be able through injections of synthetic hormone to produce some degree of rejuvenation, [that is] we may [be able to] postpone old age." Ruzicka, one of the world's preeminent chemists, still clung to the hope that testosterone might push back death.[8]

It was still not clear in the late 1930s what the sex hormones could and could not do. But for transsexuals, the new availability of such drugs would make all the difference. They could now self-medicate, transforming their bodies with nothing but a daily pill or a monthly injection—if they could get access to those drugs. Dillon could.

It was thanks to the pills that Dillon became a man—that is, within a few months he was able to pass among strangers. The regular dose of testosterone, along with manual labor, puffed up his shoulders. He had a bit of stubble now. His voice was growing gruff. And he'd begun to use the name Michael when he introduced himself to people. Working at the petrol pumps in a pair of coveralls, Dillon easily blended in. "Hey, boy, fill 'er up," the customers called. Out front, among strangers, Dillon became himself: the hard worker who collected the customers' ration coupons. In his grease-monkey suit, he hurried from car to car, a man like any other. The relief was enormous.

But when he left the pumps and went to work inside the garage—among men who knew his secret—that was another matter entirely. The mechanics and car-parkers jabbed their thumbs in his direction and guffawed, "You see that fellow over there? Well, he's not a man, he's a girl." Dillon became the butt of jokes that repeated tunelessly all day long and echoed in his head at night.

A deaf foreman ran the repair shop. For a while, he was the only one who treated Dillon as a regular bloke—because he didn't know. But Dillon's tormentors could not leave the old man out of the fun. One of them scrawled a message on a pad of paper, handed it to the foreman, and they all watched as he puzzled over the inscription. Then he studied Dillon and, after a heartbeat of delay, joined in the laughter.

Just when Dillon started his job, war came to Bristol. German planes roared over the city at night. Sirens wailed. Incendiary bombs crashed into churches and shops, and flames leapt up, blazing through roofs. On Regent Street, burning Christmas cards circled in the air, spreading sparks; by morning, the whole street had been reduced to ashes. The shells of buildings—strewn with shrapnel, scraps of furniture, and charred bodies—still exhaled wisps of smoke. Ambulances darted around uselessly.

The Germans intended to level Bristol because of its ports and airplane factories. Residents wore metal bracelets printed with their names and addresses, so that if their bodies were burned beyond recognition, they could still be identified. Because of the constant threat of explosions, local businesses began to hire "fire watchers," guards who slept on the premises through the night, ready to wake up at the first howl of an air-raid siren. Fire watchers battled encroaching flames, using whatever they could find—dirt or tires or blankets—to pile on top of the conflagrations and steer them away from buildings.

Fire didn't scare Dillon, and he desperately needed extra money and a free place to stay. So he volunteered to watch the garage at night, sleeping on the floor of the office.

When Christmas came, Dillon offered to spend the holiday in the garage, watching for bombs. He had nowhere else to go, certainly not Folkestone, where they still called him Laura. Instead, he spent Christmas alone, puttering around among tires and tools, in the bleak light that filtered through blackout shades.

The garage contained barrels of gasoline, sometimes as much as a thousand gallons. Should a spark from a German incendiary device hit the building, the whole place could explode in flames. The boss had advertised for a partner to help Dillon, but no one answered the ad; it was too dangerous a job to attract any takers.

Luckily for Dillon, the garage never took a direct hit. But bombs did explode nearby. When he heard a crash anywhere in the neighborhood, he would rush out into the street and help other fire watchers extinguish them. He didn't bother to wear his tin hat, because he was so miserable he thought he might as well die. Better, he thought, to be a dead hero than a living outcast.

During his nighttime vigils, Dillon kept his mind occupied by scribbling in his crabbed handwriting. He had begun to study medical books that summarized the recent, stunning breakthroughs in the use of hormones. Dillon took notes on his reading and then elaborated on the themes, spinning out his own theories. His notes would eventually lead to his groundbreaking book, *Self.* To become the man he wanted to be, Michael Dillon would have to do more than just dose himself on testosterone. He would have to invent the very idea of a transsexual—a person who used hormones to change his sex and then lived happily ever after.

One winter's day in 1940, Dillon found a teenage boy with a tumble of blond curls hanging around the garage office, waiting for the boss to come back from lunch. The boy, Gilbert Barrow, had just arrived from Swansea. That word alone told the whole tale, why Gilbert had washed up here and why he needed a job: the port town in Wales had just been pummeled by a maelstrom of bombs that had obliterated several city blocks and killed hundreds.

Barrow had grown up in the Muller Homes, an orphanage in Bristol, where he'd been beaten and starved; now he'd been orphaned again in Swansea—every one of his coworkers had been killed. He had nowhere to live and nothing to lose.

Dillon decided this qualified Barrow to become his partner in fire-watching, and to live in the garage office with him. Barrow happily agreed—no one else had offered to take care of him, and so he immediately clung to Dillon as a best friend. Now, every night when the other workers drifted home, the two young men pulled down the blackout shades in the garage office and waited for the bombs to fall.

On quiet nights, when they grew bored of the radio, Dillon would pace back and forth and lecture Gilbert in his Oxford accent, going on about philosophy and theology. Once he finally had an audience—this boy who listened raptly to his disquisitions—Dillon could not seem to shut up. Gilbert called Dillon's lectures "stuffshirt nonsense," but that was only teasing; he had never received a proper education, and Dillon's speeches introduced him to Plato and Aristotle, to the Socratic method and the life of the mind.

On other nights, the announcer on the nine-o'clock news would warn of bombing raids, and then the sirens would go off. The two friends would try to snatch some sleep, curled up side by side on the floor. They might wake up to screams and the tinkle of falling glass, to explosions and the whoosh of flames.

One night, a bomb erupted somewhere down the street. Bareheaded, Dillon hurried toward the door. Gilbert Barrow pleaded with him to put on his tin safety hat. Dillon had hardly used the thing, but now, at Gilbert's insistence, he shoved it on.

Pieces of paper were falling from the sky. White sheets circled and fluttered around, like propaganda. A bomb had hit John Wright's printing press at the end of the block.

Dillon darted up a flight of stairs, into the storeroom where the boss kept the tires; he rolled these down the stairs. Come down, come down, Gilbert yelled up to his friend, as flames from the neighboring building began to lick up the stairs of the garage toward Dillon. Dillon bolted down the stairs and jumped through the flames; then he and Gilbert grabbed and pushed at the tires, piling them into a fire line. Just after they finished, a second bomb blew through the roof of the printing shop, and the tires flew into the air and came raining down again. Somehow, Dillon and Barrow survived. In the morning, the boss gave them a small bonus: hardship pay. Though he'd been barred from the military, Dillon had finally gotten a chance to prove his bravery—though, of course, no one but Gilbert had seen.

One fall day, Gilbert received his call-up papers from the navy. He packed his meager possessions, ready to report for duty in Plymouth the next day. With Gilbert's departure impending, Dillon worked up the courage to allude to the awkward subject that had thickened the air between them all these months.

The garage hands must have told you I was a woman, Dillon said.

Of course they did, Gilbert replied. He'd figured out Dillon's secret on the very first day, he said, but it had never stopped him from recognizing Dillon as a man. In fact, Gilbert had told the garage hands that his friend was as much a man as any of them, which baffled the tormentors. Then Gilbert had threatened to punch any of the garage hands who called Dillon a girl. He confessed all this to Dillon now, laughing at his own bravado. And then, the next day, he left.

With his only friend gone in the fall of 1941, Dillon felt himself descending back into despair. He didn't see how he could leave the garage. To find a new job, he'd have to show his driver's license, then go through the foot-shuffling ordeal of explaining that, yes, he really was Laura Dillon. Everywhere he went, his identity papers would dog him, making it impossible for him to establish himself as a born male. It did not occur to Dillon that he could petition to the government to change his legal status. As far as Dillon knew, there was simply no way to delete the F on his documents. The letter was tattooed onto his birth certificate, seemingly as impossible to erase as a scar.

*　*　*

The earliest technology that people used to change their sex was not hormones or surgery. It was clothing: skirts and trousers, jackets, scarves, earrings, scabbards. In the nineteenth century, a delicate-looking man did not have to ask anyone's permission to become a woman: he could simply move to a new town, costume himself in gowns and rings, and find a job as a seamstress. Meanwhile, a number of women escaped poverty by melting into an army or taking up the life of a sailor. References to such "female men" pepper the newspapers of the 1800s. "Amongst the crew of the Queen Charlotte [ship] . . . was a female African who had served as a seaman in the royal navy for upwards of eleven years," according to one report. The woman, known as William Brown, "has served for some time as the captain of the fore-top, highly to the satisfaction of the officers . . . She says she is a married woman and went to sea in consequence of a quarrel with her husband . . . She declares her intention of again entering the service as a volunteer."[9]

But that kind of do-it-yourself sex change had become nearly impossible by the 1940s, when Michael Dillon wanted to switch. Years before, governments had begun tracking citizens as they changed address—and now just about every major transaction, from getting paid to buying property, required an identity card or driver's license. The military, which had once admitted men with hardly a glance at their bodies, now required recruits to parade naked before medical examiners. At the same time, governments had no legal mechanism for recognizing the transformation of a man into a woman or vice versa.

The "sex-change operation" therefore was more than just a product of medical breakthroughs that could stunningly retool the body. It was also a mid-twentieth century cultural invention, necessary in a new world of computer databases and routine medical exams. During the 1950s and 1960s, the sex-change operation would become a rite of passage that allowed a small number of people to be reclassified from male to female, and occasionally, from female to male.

In the 1940s, however, only a handful of people had ever managed to convince their government to change the sex listed on their birth certificate or passport. Dillon, certainly, had never heard of such a thing. He believed he would always be ensnared in Laura Dillon's documents.

As much as he might loathe the garage, as much as it had become his dank, oily hell, at least he earned a measure of freedom. The boss promoted him to tow-truck driver, allowing Dillon to roam around Bristol. With his Oxford accent and his upper-crust manners, Dillon got along better with the customers than he did with any of the other garage attendants. He was also the hardest worker in the shop: two decades later, Dillon could still remember the license-plate numbers of the regular customers.

Now that Dillon had become the public face of the garage, delivering cars and negotiating payments, he could no longer go under the name Miss Dillon. It only confused the patrons. And so, simply out of a concern for his business, the boss declared that from now on Miss Dillon would be called he. The other workers had to treat Dillon as a man—but only so long as customers were around.

The nights turned silent, or what passes for silent in the city during the war. In the garage, Dillon pushed piles of keys and receipts aside and went to work again on the manuscript that he'd started two years before. With Gilbert gone, he had no one to lecture, and so he poured his thoughts onto the page. He'd managed to amass a library of books on endocrinology, and he quoted liberally from these, and also from a few rare pamphlets on homosexuality and perversions he'd smuggled out of bookstores; they were all slim books, as if the authors were ashamed to have taken on the topic at all. He wrote with hands stained by oil. He smelled of petrol and pipe smoke. He had no medical training, of course. Nonetheless, he was penning a scientific book of stunning originality. He argued for medical practices that were decades ahead of their time.

In *Self*, Dillon asserted that there's only one way to determine whether a person is male or female: ask that person. True sex may have nothing to do with the appearance of the body; rather, the sense of being male, female, or something in between results from a "psychological build," according to Dillon.[10]

He posited that transsexuals develop their identities while they are still in the womb, and that aside from their desire to switch physical sex, they are perfectly ordinary. "The child would seem to develop naturally enough if only he belonged to the other sex," Dillon wrote.[11] He criticized psychiatrists for their ignorant belief that people could be talked out of a core identity—this kind of therapy was worse than useless, because it prevented transsexuals from obtaining what they really needed: surgery and hormones. Dillon argued that patients themselves, not doctors, should have the final say about their bodies. "Is it not for the individual to judge whether he should be 'mutilated,' experimented on or left alone?"[12] he wrote, arguing for a new kind of medical practice in which the patient would be the boss. If an operation or a pill could help the patient achieve "a tolerably happy life," then the patient should be given the option. "Is not this an end worth striving after?"[13] he asked rhetorically.

Today, such ideas have become our truths: in the West, millions of people every year undergo cosmetic surgeries to look prettier and younger, or to sculpt their bodies into the shape that conforms to their aspirations. But in Dillon's day, these procedures were rare. Before World War II, Britain had only one plastic surgeon; in the United States, there were only a handful.

At the same time, thousands of people endured their own mysterious urges in silence and confusion, wrestling with the compulsion to cross-dress as they fought to fake their way through life in bodies that shamed them. Most would-be transsexuals in the 1940s had no idea that transformation was possible, or that others suffered as they did.

As Dillon scrawled out his theories in that garage, about a hundred miles away in Coventry, an army captain was undergoing a battery of tests to prove he could join Britain's elite team of fliers. The young captain half-believed that if he could escape into the sky, if he could break through the sound barrier, then he might be able to conquer the compulsions that tormented him. Unlike Michael Dillon, this young man did not know how to explain his strange urges. For now, he was doing everything he could to pretend they didn't exist.

In 1941, Robert Cowell stood in front of a board of medical examiners, balancing with one leg up in the air and his eyes shut. The twenty-three-year-old had applied to become a pilot in the Royal Air Force, and now, with a team of doctors watching, he had to pass a series of tests to prove that he could fly a one-seat plane into battle without getting airsick, dizzy, or light-headed.

Within ten years, this seeming paragon of British manhood would transform himself into a curvy blonde: Roberta Cowell. But if you study early photos of Robert Cowell during his military career—he poses in an army uniform or with racing goggles pushed up onto his forehead—it's hard to find any foreshadowing of the woman he would become. He looks young and brash, with an arch smile, as if he's about to mutter some droll comment. Years later, Roberta Cowell would claim that she had been born a hermaphrodite, or a man with a feminine body. But if there was any trace of femininity in Robert Cowell back in 1941, the Royal Air Force medical examiners did not detect it; they did not discover nascent breasts when they examined the young man's chest for tumors, nor did they find genital anomalies when they palpated his groin for hernias. Cowell's military identity card noted only one defect on his body—"scar under chin"—and the accompanying photo shows him as an intense young man with close-set eyes. The RAF accepted him as a fighter pilot.

Under his flying jacket, that young man wore a talisman around his neck—a tiny vial of hot-rod fuel affixed to a chain. He liked to open it up and breathe in the smell of fuel, the perfume of velocity. Cowell had begun racing cars as a teenager, rattling around tracks at top speed with his teeth chattering. He was happiest when the world blurred around him, trees and clouds and faces softened by speed. And because he loved to go fast, to push past limits, he volunteered to fly RAF planes at an altitude of forty thousand feet—at the very rim of the atmosphere, so high that he once nearly passed out from oxygen starvation.

He survived bullets whistling by his ears, crashes, a broken altimeter, all of it proof of his luck. The constant danger delighted him, and the Spitfire planes he jockeyed "were all I had hoped for, and more."[14] Then one day his luck ended.

On his very last mission against the Germans, a piece of flak ripped into the hull of his plane. The engine sputtered and went silent. The plane plummeted. Cowell readied himself to jump out and yank his parachute cord, but the ground was rushing up too fast for that. He crash-landed somewhere east of the Rhine. When he crawled out of the wreck—miraculously alive—he found German soldiers standing over him.

Cowell became a prisoner of war in Stalag Luft I. He had always lived for the blur of speed, that softening of edges when he roared past trees and buildings. Now he was stuck behind barbed wire, a prisoner in slow-motion hell. Rats crawled over his body with precise little pats of their paws. German guards wore scimitars of dirt under their nails. A piece of bread glittered with beautiful crumbs that turned out to be broken glass—the Stalag cook had gone crazy and tried to kill the prisoners. Once, when the Red Cross packages failed to arrive, Cowell became so desperate for food that he chased down the prison cats, killed them, and ate them raw. "There is very little that you cannot eat if you are hungry enough."[15] He saw a prisoner shot down for drunkenness; his best friend in the camp went mad; and Cowell lost fifty pounds. Through it all, he retreated from his surroundings by fantasizing about what he'd do after the war ended. While he huddled in the mud, an image took shape in his mind: a twelve-cylinder engine with Aspin rotary valves. As soon as he was free, he decided, he would build that engine, drop it into a race car, and enter it in the Grand Prix.[16]

He must also have thought about the woman inside him, must have felt Roberta beginning to assert herself. But a prisoner-of-war camp is no place to nurture taboo urges. And so he dreamed of engines.

CHAPTER 4
SIR HAROLD'S SCALPEL

O N   A   S U M M E R ' S   D A Y   I N   1942, Dillon strolled the promenade at an English beach town. He wore a sport coat, flannel trousers, and a clean-shaven face. Much as he loved to swim, he would not have risked putting on a pair of bathing trunks to dive into the ocean. He'd fled from the garage for a weekend holiday, but his problems had come with him. He still had breasts. He described those fleshy appendages—which had withered after years of exposure to testosterone—as "persistent," as if they had a will of their own.

That morning, as he walked past the gaudy awnings and the bathers, Dillon began to feel dizzy. Suddenly, everything went dark. He had passed out, his head crashing into the wood of the boardwalk.

When he woke up, he found himself in the local hospital with a doctor peering at him. This was the first of two incidents that would change Dillon's life.

The doctor wanted to know his name.

"Laura Dillon," he said. And when the doctor refused to believe he was a woman, Dillon reached into his pocket and produced an ID: Laura Dillon, it said. Ignoring the ID, the doctor ordered the patient wheeled off to the men's ward. His dizziness, Dillon would later learn, had been caused by hypoglycemia; he had passed out because his blood sugar had suddenly dropped.

That night, German planes roared over the town. Dillon lay in the dark, his head bandaged, watching incendiaries light up the sky and distant buildings burst into flame. By morning, the ward had filled with injured men. "I felt as if I were a being from another world, quite unconnected with this carnage," he wrote later.[1] He was in a men's ward but still not a man.

It would take Dillon weeks to recuperate from the blow to his head, and for what? He'd return to that dungeon of a garage, where the other workers hated him, to the humiliating mess of living in the twilight between the sexes.

Six months later, back in Bristol, an enormously lucky thing happened: Dillon blacked out again, this time on a city street. He crumpled to the ground and smacked his skull. Passersby carried him to the Royal Infirmary. After the doctor had treated Dillon's head injury, he set to work seeing what he could do about the *other* problem: the breasts. Dillon had avoided medical men ever since the encounter with Foss, but the doctors at the Royal Infirmary proved to be entirely different. There, he met a physician who introduced himself as "plastic surgeon." It's likely Dillon had never before heard the term. Only a few dozen doctors in the world practiced under the *plastic surgeon* label; in the early 1940s, they were a small, maligned cadre of physicians, still regarded as quacks, and they scandalized their colleagues with their willingness to cater to their patients' desires.

The plastic surgeon agreed to give Dillon a double mastectomy and to introduce him to Sir Harold Gillies, the only surgeon in Britain who might be able and willing to turn Dillon's female genitals into a penis. Plastic surgeons, it turned out, saw Dillon's problem exactly as Dillon did. He was trapped in the wrong body. And so he needed to change that body. It was that simple.

In the early twentieth century, if you were born with a port-wine stain blooming red across your cheek, or if cancer left you with a face so mangled that you regularly got ejected from restaurants for frightening the other diners, or if you'd lost a breast or were burned

Harold Gillies as a young surgeon during World War I.

beyond recognition, you would resign yourself to your deformities. Reconstructive surgery was still in its infancy. Patients weren't reconstructed so much as they were patched up. In cases where doctors needed to sew up a hole in a patient's cheek, they did so with as much finesse as if they were upholstering a sofa.

During the First World War, British soldiers returned from the front with their noses gone, jaws exploded, entire faces a mass of bone and bloody gristle; trench war protected their torsos, but left their heads exposed to gunshots. Survivors sometimes wore masks to spare others from seeing the holes, the wounds, the chinless mouths, the dead eyes.

It was Harold Gillies—a skinny, thirty-three-year-old surgeon—who in 1916 convinced the War Office to set up a wing in a military hospital dedicated to repairing faces. Recognizing that no one had *heard* of plastic surgery, Gillies decided to advertise his new clinic: at the stationery store, he printed up labels with the address of his hospital ward, and he sent these out to the front lines; the mangled soldiers would wear the address labels, like so many human packages, and eventually find their way to Gillies. It was the first of Gillies's many PR efforts on behalf of plastic surgery.

He'd learned a little of his art from a German textbook and a bit more from a brilliant French surgeon who'd let him watch a single operation. But mostly, Gillies made up plastic surgery as he went along, smoking furiously, operating for a dozen hours a day, sketching noses on the backs of envelopes. According to one nurse who worked under Gillies, he treated a "stream of wounded, men with half their faces literally blown to pieces, with the skin left hanging in shreds and the jawbones crushed to a pulp that felt like sand under your fingers. 'Don't worry, sonny, you'll be all right and have as good a face as most of us before we're finished with you,' Captain Gillies would say."[2]

The tools he depended upon to save their faces were crude. The smell of ether and chloroform stunk up the surgical theater—it leaked out of the patient's mouth, and doctors and nurses often worked in a fog of it, half-anesthetized themselves. He used a centuries-old surgical technique for moving skin around; for instance, he would cut a flap of skin in the forehead, leaving one end of the flap anchored. He would then rotate the flap so it covered the nose area. Gillies used a similar technique to transfer skin from the chest or shoulders to the face; one end of the skin flap would draw blood from the old location while the other end took root in the new location over weeks. The technique had many drawbacks: the underside of the skin could dry out, scab over, or flare up with deadly infection.

In 1917, while he was peeling skin off a sailor's shoulder, Gillies noticed how the edges of the flap tended to curl inward, the way paper curls when it's held up to a candle. He realized that there was a much better way to move skin around the body: he would let the flap of skin curl in on itself and then sew it into a tube, sealing off the inner side from the air. These tubes of skin, or "suitcase handles," could grow on the patient's body for weeks at a time; they could be moved about, end over end, across the body until they reached their final destination; or they could stretch like stalks to wherever you needed the flesh. The "tube pedicle," as Gillies called it, revolutionized surgery: suddenly, the body had turned modular. A U-shaped handle of flesh could be grown on the chest and moved to the face to form a nose; an extra roll hanging off the stomach could become a penis.

Gillies and his colleagues had entirely changed the field of plastic surgery, but when the First World War ended, so, too, did the government's support for these treatments. The art fell back into obscurity. When Gillies traveled to the United States to talk to his colleagues there, some of the world's top plastic surgeons met in the basement of a Minnesota house—they were literally an underground group. Gillies knew he'd have to mount "a long stubborn fight to obtain the recognition and rightful position of plastic surgery."[3]

In the early 1920s, Harold Gillies became the first plastic surgeon to set up a private practice in Britain. "Name plate up. Secretary installed. Now all I want is a few patients willing to place themselves in the hands of a surgeon crazy enough to nail his fortune—and that of his wife and four children—to the mast of plastic surgery. To venture into this new field is certainly a gamble," he wrote.[4] At first, most of the patients who consulted him had survived burns, or farm accidents or car crashes; but Gillies also did a brisk business in turning A cups into D cups, as well as other cosmetic surgeries.

In 1922, a young maidservant plodded into Gillies's consulting room with "great lumbering strides, lifted a hairy leg and vaulted onto the couch like a Rugby player." After an examination, Gillies diagnosed the problem: the woman was actually a man. The patient suffered from hypospadias, a condition in which the opening of the urethra appears on the shaft of the penis or near the scrotum rather than on the tip; largely a cosmetic problem, hypospadias can cause the penis to look vagina-like. Therefore, baby boys with the condition are sometimes mislabeled girls.

Gillies performed minor surgery to correct the problem; more important, he provided the young man with a diagnosis that allowed for a legal sex change. A week after the surgery, the "young man left the hospital to work as a manservant instead of as a maid." Eventually, "he married a farmer's daughter."[5]

Today, surgeons routinely operate on infants with hypospadias, often for solely cosmetic reasons—the penis doesn't look "normal" to them. It's a practice that has become controversial in the last decade. Cosmetic operations on both the penis and the vagina can result in long-term side effects: numbing, scarring, and sexual dysfunction. Groups such as the Intersex Society of North America argue that cosmetic surgery performed on infants is tantamount to genital mutilation and should be outlawed.

In Gillies's day, however, these operations were rarely performed on infants; instead, people who were born with ambiguous genitals grew up unaltered and—sometimes—ended up in Gillies's office seeking help. Gillies developed a reputation for treating adults who'd "been put in the wrong sex bin," as he called it. Hypospadias was a catch-all diagnosis he used for patients who'd been designated "female" at birth but who possessed ambiguous genitals and preferred to be men. Using this legal diagnosis, he quietly changed his patients' sex. For now, he did not attempt the near-impossible feat of turning a vagina into a penis; he affected only minor changes, and only on female patients with ambiguous genitals.

There is no record of Gillies treating male-to-female transsexuals during this period; to do so, he would have had to amputate healthy testicles, which was a violation of the mayhem statute, a law still on the books in Britain and the United States. In Gillies's consulting room, sex was a one-way street. You could only go from female to male.

*   *   *

By the 1930s, Gillies—who had once despaired of ever making a living at plastic surgery—had become the highest-paid doctor on posh Harley Street, pulling in as much as thirty thousand pounds a year making women (and a few men) gorgeous. Other physicians might look down on Gillies for catering to patients' whims, might scorn him as a mere beauty doctor, but the patients themselves beat a path to Gillies's door. They knew he was the best man for breasts and eyebrows and noses. With almost no competition in his field, Gillies could charge a fortune to prop up the sagging edifice of a rich woman's face.

But plenty of times he offered his services for free. Gillies particularly delighted in helping people who had been ill-treated by society. He could use his scalpel to correct social wrongs; he could reverse a patient's fortunes in a few hours. People with syphilis, for instance, wore the evidence of their sexual histories on their faces. Within an afternoon, Gillies could erase the telltale "saddle nose" of the syphilitic, turning an outcast with the flattened nose into an ordinary man or woman. "It sets one furiously to think. What influence has our appearance on our character and on our social reactions?" Gillies wrote. "The link between the psyche and the surgeon becomes more and more evident."

He told the tale of one young woman who showed up in his office with breasts hanging down to her belly. Almost every other surgeon in the 1930s would have refused to operate on her. Gillies took four pounds off each of her breasts. "There was no medical reason for the operation," he argued, but wasn't the girl's suffering reason enough?[6]

"My view of whether a cosmetic operation is justifiable is clear. If it is going to make a great difference to the patient in happiness, in social advancement, and particularly in a job, it is justified. If it gives real happiness, that is the most that any surgeon or medicine can give," he wrote.[7] Gillies made happiness a reason for surgery—which in turn upended the traditional relationship between doctor and patient. The doctor could no longer pretend to know what was best; he would have to listen to the patient to find out.

Despite the controversial nature of some of the surgeries he performed, by the mid-1930s Gillies's technical innovations—and his advocacy on behalf of wounded soldiers and children with birth defects—won him acclaim. In the 1930s, after he was knighted by the king of England, invitations crammed his mailbox. He was now expected to speak to crowds of notables at black-tie affairs.

Gillies had always been a prankster, and these formal dinners brought out his impish side. At ceremonies in his honor, Gillies would crawl under the table and hide, while overhead the emcee rattled off an introduction to the eminent surgeon. When the spotlight swung over to Gillies's chair, it would be empty.

Gillies spent almost as much time dreaming up practical jokes as he did mapping out new surgeries. Even as a middle-aged workaholic with a two-pack-a-day cigarette habit, Gillies found time to invent a gag toilet-roll dispenser—it played a ditty every time the unsuspecting user gave it a spin. Once, he showed up for a golf game wearing a fake beard and ridiculous knickerbockers, claiming to be "Dr. Scroggie of South Africa"; he persisted in the ruse until one of his friends yanked off the beard.

Other people might agonize about the ethical questions posed by plastic surgery. Not Gillies. He regarded the flesh as so much costume. He pasted patrician noses on threadbare soldiers. He tightened up acres of foreheads. He reduced a female golfer's breasts to give her a better swing; and then, when her lover complained, Gillies rebuilt the breasts again. He regarded pieces of flesh as if they were fake beards or funny hats; the tube pedicle, that bag of skin he could move anywhere on the body, was his whoopee cushion. Plastic surgery might itself be considered the grandest and sweetest of his pranks. He disguised his patients as the people they wanted to be.

For Gillies, the 1930s was a blur of face-lifts, false mustaches, gala dinners, and golf games. Then war broke out—"ghastly news from Europe," he wrote in 1939—and the Ministry of Health called on him to create a special hospital to treat face wounds, in anticipation of the blitzes and the battles to come.[8] Gillies took over an abandoned hospital building in the English countryside, a place called Rooksdown, and outfitted it with the latest surgical equipment. Finding a staff proved difficult: plastic surgeons were so scarce in Britain that he was able to lure only one other Englishman to join him. Even in the United States—the country already so enamored of beauty treatments—only sixty plastic surgeons were practicing at the start of World War II.[9]

Dillon was lucky to encounter a plastic surgeon in the early 1940s, when so few of them existed. The doctor at the Bristol hospital—whom Dillon does not name—had studied under Gillies, of course. He no doubt knew about Gillies's treatments for "hypospadias"—the diagnosis that had already allowed several female patients to change their birth certificates and become male.

"Why not get reregistered?" the plastic surgeon asked Dillon that day in the Bristol hospital.

It had never occurred to Dillon that he could change his legal sex. "Reregistration? Was it possible?" Dillon wondered. "Every way I had turned I had seemed to be hemmed in by birth certificates, identity cards, driving licenses and my mail as it was addressed to [Laura Dillon]." Because of the documents, he could not take a job as a man, could not start up a new life without his secret coming out. But a new legal identity would fix that—and plastic surgeons turned out to be the kind of doctors who knew how to navigate the legal system. "It was as if a sudden tiny gleam of light had appeared showing a possible line of escape."[10]

Months later, Dillon dashed into the Labor Exchange with a doctor's note, hiding his panic under an expression of blank calm. He was terrified that the clerk might ridicule him or, worse, refuse to cooperate. Instead, the man behind the counter looked over the documents and stamped them with a bored thump, thump, thump.

That's how, in a matter of moments in 1943, Laura Maud Dillon became Lawrence Michael Dillon.

CHAPTER 5

WITH GIRLS ONE HAS TO BE CAREFUL

THE WORLD BEGAN TO SEEM WORTH LIVING IN AFTER ALL," Dillon wrote of that giddy period when he was first able to saunter down the street as a legally recognized man, flash his papers, tip his hat, sign his new name. "It was the first time I was able to start among people who knew nothing whatever about me and accepted me as an ordinary man. The relief was indescribable."[1] And yet, he was still far from being free of his history as Laura. His records from Oxford, for instance, would be impossible to explain to a new employer: he'd graduated from an all-women's college at the university.

And then there was the matter of his personal story. All of us carry around a mini-autobiography, little scenes from our lives that we present to strangers like photos in a billfold to let them know who we are. I played rugby as a lad. I was stationed in France. I fancied the waitress and so I married her. Dillon would have to construct this kind of history for his new, male self. He would have to acquire a credible life story, a new set of academic records, and—to finalize the transition—a penis.

Acquiring that escutcheon between his legs had become an obsession for Dillon. How could he ask a girl to a dance when he still hid female genitalia under his trousers? How could he join a rowing team and shower with his mates? And what if he passed out again on the street, banged his head, and was carried into another hospital?

Would they put him in the men's ward or the women's ward? His legal papers named him as male; his body told another story. As long as he lived with this inconsistency, he would suffer the torment of what-ifs.

So in 1943, Dillon took a day off from the garage and traveled to a small town called Basingstoke; there, he walked up a country lane to the rambling hospital, Rooksdown, and into hallways crowded with soldiers. Some hobbled around with cocoons of bandages around their heads; others wore their wounds out in the open, two holes where the nose should be, a clawed piece of flesh instead of a chin, or tubes of skin running between shoulder and cheek.

Dillon had come here to meet with Harold Gillies, one of the most eminent plastic surgeons in the world—which at this point still did not mean much, since there were so few of them. Dillon might have expected a dashing hero with a film-star face; Gillies turned out to be just the opposite. In a shabby consulting room, Dillon found a stoop-shouldered, moth-eaten geezer with a horseshoe of white hair clinging to his otherwise bald head, a cigarette smoldering between the V of two fingers. Gillies looked even more disheveled than usual. He'd been operating around the clock, sleeping in spurts of three or four hours. And still, as fast as he could clean up the faces and the hands, more soldiers poured in, truckloads of them, just in from the front.

Gillies promised to help Dillon—but not yet. The Rooksdown surgeons could not possibly clear up time in the operating room until after the war ended. Then, if Dillon continued to want it, Gillies promised to give him a penis. The surgeon had built plenty of penises before—he'd learned his techniques by working on men who'd had their genitals shot off in the trenches, or those who had never had any to begin with. "In Bob's case, there was no penis, but two perfectly normal testicles in their scrotum that sat forlornly over the pubis," Gillies wrote of a high school football player.[2] The

Sir Harold Gillies consults with the matron of Rooksdown in 1949 or 1950. *From the archives of the British Association of Plastic Surgeons*

poor boy often had to use women's bathrooms because he could not stand up to urinate. The surgeon built a penis for him from a tube of flesh harvested from his body.

No one had ever attempted to transform female genitals into a penis, but Gillies didn't see why he couldn't. Dillon's case, when you got right down to it, was not so different from Bob's—at least from a surgical standpoint. But from an ethical and political standpoint, well, Dillon's operation would be unprecedented. Gillies had operated on women with ambiguous genitals before, helping to redesignate them as men; but this would be the first true sex-change operation in England. If word got out, a scandal would ensue.

Gillies had already been beat up enough by the newspapers, thank you very much. "I know only too well how much harm unwanted Press publicity is doing not only to our plastic surgery in general but to me in particular," Gillies wrote in 1941.[3] And so, he made sure that no one would find out that he was performing a sex change. He diagnosed Dillon as an "acute hypospadic"—in the medical records, Dillon would look like a biological man who'd checked into the hospital for a cosmetic repair of his penis.

But not yet. Gillies could not begin working on Dillon until the beds in Rooksdown cleared out. "To wait with hope in one's heart is easy," Dillon wrote. "So back I went to study science and to park cars."[4]

Already he was plotting his escape from that awful existence, from the men in coveralls who pointed their thumbs at him and the stink of petrol and the nights curled into a corner to sleep.

But where would he go to make a fresh start? He needed to find a place to hide out while he was still half-formed and learning how to pass. For Dillon, the answer was simple: academia. He would incubate himself at a university, where he could generate a new set of records for himself, as Michael Dillon; and, in the chaos of campus life, he could also test-drive maleness and learn to navigate his way through a frightening array of new situations: dancing with girls, rowing on a men's team, ordering a whiskey at a pub, and chumming around with ex-servicemen.

And what would he study? As a girl Laura had imagined herself as a missionary, an explorer, or an American Indian; she'd pored over boys' adventure books, and it had always seemed to her that her future lay across the sea, in Africa particularly. But instead of traveling, Dillon had spent most of adult life with his nose in books. He'd learn everything he could about hormones and how they affected the body; he'd almost finished writing his own book, which included a primer on endocrinology, from the pineal gland to ovarian tumors. He'd used his body as a laboratory, testing out pills and dosages. He knew more about testosterone than most doctors. He had become an explorer of the body, of skin and hair growth and muscle. He began to think about medical school.

Dillon—who'd never had a proper father—now regarded Sir Harold Gillies as his role model. Though the surgeon might appear worn-down and a bit portly these days, in his youth Gillies had represented Dillon's beau ideal of masculinity. He'd been an intellect and an athlete, a natural at everything he tried. Gillies had attended Cambridge University, where he'd rowed his team to glory during his undergraduate years; he'd served as a heroic doctor in the war; he was a top golfer on the amateur circuit and a skilled fly fisherman. Everything seemed to come easily to Gillies, as it never had to Dillon.

Most of all, though, Dillon felt gratitude. In some brand-new, twentieth-century sense, Gillies was about to become his father. Soon, on the operating-room table, he would fashion Dillon into the shape he should have had all along. "To Sir Harold, the making of life normal again for those who were mutilated, whether by man or by nature, was all-important," Dillon wrote later. "It was to this he devoted his life and it was to this that I owed mine."[5]

And so Dillon decided he would train himself to be a doctor—to follow Gillies's model.

Applying to medical school, however, would mean he'd have to alter that trail of records that marked him as a former female. A beloved tutor at Oxford, Jimmy McKie, helped him fill out applications, even working a bit of bureaucratic magic. McKie convinced the Oxford university registrar to strike out "Laura Maud Dillon," who'd graduated from St. Anne's College, and replace her with L. M. Dillon, who graduated from the all-male Brasenose College. Thus, Dillon accomplished an academic sex change.

He applied to Trinity College, in Dublin, and got in; the medical program seemed perfect. Not only was it affiliated with Oxford— and anything connected with the school felt like home to him— but it also embraced a hands-on approach to training. At Trinity, the students trailed doctors, treated patients, and even assisted with operations—a blood-and-guts education that Dillon craved after so many years buried in books.

There was only one problem with the university: it sat twenty-six miles away from the Dillon family estate in county Meath, Ireland, where Bobby had ensconced himself among the local foxhunters and gentlemen farmers, every bit the young baronet. Dillon and his brother had not seen each other for seven years; Bobby had made it clear that Laura (the name he still insisted on calling his sibling) should scuttle away, leave the family alone, and by all means do no more to besmirch the proud Dillon name. Bobby would never recognize Dillon as a man, and certainly not as a brother.

Nonetheless, Bobby could hardly forbid his sibling from living in Ireland. So the two of them met at a restaurant to discuss the matter. Michael proposed that they strike up a new relationship—they could visit each other on occasion and call each other "cousin." Surely, no one in Ireland would ever suspect that he had been Bobby's sister.

Bobby refused. He regarded Dillon as a woman in a suit and announced he would never again see her. He'd agreed to lunch only so as to issue new rules of engagement: Laura must never advertise her connection to the Dillons of Lismullen; she should never show up at the family estate; and, above all, she must avoid publicity. If she ended up in the tabloids again, she'd bring them all down.

Dillon sized up his brother—who seemed so humiliated to be related to a freak, so desperate to cling to his reputation as the proper squire—and agreed to Bobby's rules. So, he had a brother no more. Nor could he go home to visit the aunts. Dillon had once risked sneaking into Folkestone in 1945 or 1946, just after the war, to prepare the house for the aunts' return—they'd fled Folkestone because of the Blitz. He'd slunk up through the overgrown yard, let himself into the house, and slept in the living room, alone. He'd come home to work only: to clean up the place, make some repairs, hack away at the jungle in the yard until it looked presentable. Aunt Toto was not above ordering her nephew to serve as her handyman, but she was afraid to be seen near him. Until the late 1940s, she forbid him from visiting Folkestone again.

Dillon agreed that visiting Folkestone might be dangerous. One gossipy neighbor could leak his story—and then everything he'd worked for would be ruined. He'd be treated as a monster again, a false man, an exhibition piece.

This meant that he started his career as a medical student with no family and no home to go back to during the holidays. He was becoming himself, but the cost of his new identity was extraordinarily high: many of the people who had loved Laura had no use for Michael.

In the late 1980s, the journalist Liz Hodgkinson interviewed several doctors who had trained at Trinity alongside Dillon. Few of his classmates suspected that Dillon had once been female. One, Hillas Smith, was "staggered" when he discovered Dillon's secret years later. "It doesn't say much for our powers of observation that we never guessed," he said.[6]

During his first year, Dillon appears to have confessed the truth to only one of his classmates, Patricia Leeson—and even then, he dared tell her only a partial truth. Dillon left her with the impression that he'd been born male, but misclassified—perhaps because of ambiguous genitals—as female and therefore raised as a girl. "He told me that he had been brought up a woman but always felt himself to be male and was completely lost among women," according to Leeson. "I became quite friendly with him for a time, and would go back with him to his flat. He did like a female to go out with on Saturday evenings for a meal or to the pictures," according to Leeson, who regarded these outings as purely Platonic.[7]

At Trinity, he fell back into the old patterns he'd established at Oxford—he studied and he rowed. Now, of course, he belonged to a men's team. Beyond his boathouse friendships, he avoided social entanglements.

Dillon lived mostly apart and alone during medical school,

estranged from the much younger students around him, who chattered about their mums and daddies and where they would go for Christmas holidays. When they exploded out of class and headed to a pub together, he retreated to his house, behind a veil of pipe smoke. A distant relative had just died and left him a small inheritance—enough to buy a small house and to outfit himself as a proper bachelor with a den, gentleman's-club chairs, and books everywhere. On the brick mantelpiece, in lieu of family photographs, Dillon displayed pictures of himself posing with his rowing teams; in addition to the Trinity team, he'd joined a local Dublin club. The cups he'd won gleamed from the mantel. Dillon had proved himself one of the most skilled rowers at Trinity—this, despite the angry stitches under his clothes and a body that was still hovering halfway between male and female.

Despite all the loneliness and anxiety, he felt himself lucky, dazzlingly so. In early 1945, with the war nearly over, soldiers were flooding home to Britain, shedding their khakis to become fathers and sweethearts again and to try to resume their lives as ordinary men. Some of them humped along on crutches; some rolled in wheelchairs; and others bore invisible but deep scars of what they'd seen, shell-shocked men poisoned by bad dreams. And the most unfortunate of all remained in prisoner-of-war camps, waiting to be set free by the Allied forces. One of those unfortunates was Robert Cowell.

In early 1945, Cowell still languished behind the barbed wire of Stalag Luft I, emaciated and covered in scabies. He clung to a fantasy about his life after the war, a dream of "freedom, food, gaiety, safety"[8]— and of starting his own business to design an engine that would win the Grand Prix. Then, one day freedom came in the form of Allied bombers, a phalanx of B19s that peeled out of the sky and landed near the German camp. A few hours after the prison-camp gates opened, Cowell was on his way to Britain, hurling himself back to his old life, to the woman he'd married just before the war.

He settled in with his family—his wife and two small daughters he barely knew—and waited to be happy. In 1947, he partnered with a friend to start the firm of Cowell and Watson, which would create prototypes of engines. Cowell put in thousands of pounds, most of it borrowed from his parents, gambling on his own genius for design: he'd either come up with a winning engine or he'd lose all the money. In his spare time, he competed in every motor race he could, then repaired to the pubs, drinking with his fellow drivers. And, oh, the cars: Altas, Maseratis, Delahayes. He was doing exactly what he'd dreamed about when he'd shivered in the mud in Stalag Luft I. But freedom turned out to be nothing like the fantasy he'd constructed back then. Happiness eluded him.

He was gripped by an urge that would not let him go, that shamed and humiliated him. In secret, during this period, Cowell was experimenting with wigs and lipstick, skirts and bras. It's hard to know precisely when Cowell put on his first dress, when he tried on a blond wig and glimpsed his true self, Roberta, in the mirror. But by the late 1940s, the compulsion to live as a woman had begun to overwhelm him. "His male-like occupation was a mask," according to the surgeon's case study of Cowell, written up years later. "At all times, he had an intense urge to clothe himself as a female and to be admired as such. When the adventurous spirit moved him, he would risk an evening sortie." Cowell, who was short for a man and small-boned with no visible Adam's apple, discovered during these adventures that he could easily pass as an attractive woman. "His success," according to the case study, "was almost embarrassing."[9]

His marriage, which had always had "an underlying air of falseness about it," finally fell apart.[10] He separated from his wife in 1948, but that provided little relief. Roberta, his inner woman, controlled him. She demanded to exist with such urgency that there was no space in his mind for pistons and solenoids and brake lines, or even ordinary contentment. "My physical well-being disappeared . . . Something seemed drastically wrong somewhere."[11] He had fallen into a deep depression, so crippling that he could not work.

He did not know what else to do except to submit to Freudian analysis, 1940s-style therapy with all the trimmings: Oedipus complex, couch, dreams, ink blots. The results of his tests revealed, according to Cowell's analyst, that the patient's unconscious mind was "predominately female."[12]

The diagnosis should not have come as a surprise, but it plunged Cowell into a yet deeper agony. He was mortified that the psychiatrists could see the women inside him, too. He had tumbled into some netherworld between masculine and feminine; Roberta was taking over, even while his body and his voice and his legal documents remained stubbornly male. "I had not the slightest desire to swell the ranks of the gentlemen of no particular gender," he wrote.[13] But now, it seemed, he was. He could become a half-creature, a woman-man, or he could commit suicide. Those were his only choices. Or so he thought. He did not know that a third choice existed.

"In sex a woman; in natural ability a man," the surgeon, Harold Gillies, wrote about his patient Michael Dillon. He'd borrowed the line from the gravestone of Maria Theresa, the queen of Hungary and Bohemia who'd ruled with all the power of a king. Gillies was the sort of surgeon who liked to think up mottoes for his patients. He tried to find something mythic in the miserable people in his waiting room, to invent a heroic story for them, a story in which surgery was always the turning point. In his case study of Dillon, Gillies describes the patient as a talented athlete who dreamed of competing in international rowing regattas—but who needed to be able to pass as a man in the locker room to do so. Gillies celebrated the miraculous ease with which Dillon had crossed the gender line and outperformed many of his male teammates. The surgeon liked to tell upbeat stories about his patients—stories in which happiness always came to those with pinned-back ears, restored noses, firmer breasts.

It was, in Gillies's mind, just that easy. If he could only give Dillon a penis, then all of his other problems—the social awkwardness, the aloofness, the fear of women—would surely clear up.

For four years, from 1946 through 1949, Dillon would see a lot of Gillies, as he shuttled back and forth between the Trinity campus and Rooksdown, changing out of his medical-school tweeds and into a hospital gown. He proved to be an undistinguished student; but he was an outstanding candidate for surgery.

Dr. Ralph Millard, an American whom Gillies had invited to work at Rooksdown, assisted in the grueling surgeries on Dillon and so had occasion to chat with the patient a few times. He remembered Dillon as "well oriented" and a "good patient," a stiff-upper-lip fellow who would be able to endure pedicles and infections and long hours on the operating table—exactly the kind of patient you'd want if you were about to undertake a world's-first surgery. "We were excited," remembers Millard. "Gillies was undaunted . . . He knew how to charter unknown waters. He would go into a [controversial operation] without too much concern."[14]

Gillies decided to incorporate the flesh from the patient's clitoris into the base of the penis; this would preserve as much erotic sensation as possible. After the surgeries, Dillon would urinate in an entirely new way—through an artificially constructed tube that was grafted onto his own urethra and that would extend up through the length of the penis. Gillies did not plan to remove the patient's ovaries. Neither he nor Dillon explains this surgical omission in any public writings about the operation.

In 1957, Gillies and Millard would publish *The Principles and Art of Plastic Surgery*, in which Dillon appears as the case study titled "Female with Male Outlook." (By the late 1950s, sex changes were still controversial, but by then Gillies apparently felt safe enough to abandon the cover-up story that he'd concocted for Dillon—hypospadias—and admit that his patient had been born with an ordinary female body.) In a series of unflinching, close-up photographs that accompany the case study, we see Dillon from the surgeon's point of view. The first photograph shows the patient's groin: between the spread legs, we can see the crack of the buttocks, the lips of the vagina, and the nub of the clitoris; above the female genitalia, the photograph shows, jarringly, a man's hairy belly. In the next photograph, a handle of flesh hangs off a freckled man's chest—this is the tube pedicle that would eventually form the penis. Then the next photo: a woman's groin—shaved now, so it looks like a prepubescent girl's—with a sausage of flesh extending between the belly and the vagina; the tube pedicle has taken root in its new location and is ready to be moved. Next photo: the patient weeks or months after surgery, standing, his head cut off by the frame of the picture; he's shot from far away and the new penis appears as nothing more than a white blur; the pubic hair has grown back in, and his legs shine with a deep tan. There is another after photo, a close-up of the penis, emerging from a thatch of pubic hair; it resembles, in this portrait, a frankfurter, oddly fat and smooth with a large hole at its end.

Gillies had run a mast of cartilage through the center of the penis, so that it would stay semierect at all times—always ready for sexual intercourse. But it was not sex that Gillies had worried about so much as urinating. He'd lavished care on the urethra that ran through the penis, and it worked beautifully. A photograph proves this point: the penis shoots a healthy stream of urine into a pitcher.

"After initial difficulties, no trouble has been experienced with urination," Gillies notes in his case study. "Provided thus with a new organ, the patient's life has been a social success; he has become an active and successful business man and is anxious to have everything done that would make it justifiable for him to marry."[15] To

Gillies's mind, the penis had allowed his patient to live entirely as a man, and the story had ended happily ever after.

Dillon could urinate, that was true. But marriage was another, far more complicated matter for an artificial man in the 1940s. How on earth was he to court a woman?

Gillies had urged him to go out, circulate, enjoy himself, and that is what Dillon tried to do. But it was hard, women scared him. He had never been schooled in how to flirt with a woman, how to woo her. Still, when the school's Biological Association threw its annual gala dance at the end of the term, Dillon would screw up the courage to invite one of the female medical students to come with him; he enjoyed waltzing around the dance floor in his white tie and tails and had turned a little vain about how good he looked. But when the dance ended, his partner swung out of his arms and he let her flit off toward some other man.

Dillon was far too busy for girlfriends anyway. Along with a team of his fellow medical students, he would hurry to the tenements to tend to women who couldn't afford to give birth in a hospital. For hours, they'd wait beside a patient's bed, killing time before she went into the final stages of labor. They played cards. They dozed. And they chatted. Other students might gush about their families and their sweethearts, but Dillon held himself apart, a stiff presence in the corner of the room. He was more than ten years older than the others, a diffident man with broad shoulders, an elegantly trimmed goatee, and professorial stench of pipe smoke hanging about his clothes. In his final years of medical school, Dillon had come into his own physically, as if he'd taken possession of his male body and finally made it his. He grew broad-chested and big-shouldered, and he emphasized his new physique with tailored suit jackets. He had become, in a word, handsome. And that made being male all the more dangerous.

"With girls one had to be careful," Dillon wrote. "An evening's flirting at a dance was one thing and a relief—but no more."[16] As soon as the evening ended, Dillon retreated to his bachelor's house, and the young woman never heard from him again.

If the young woman grew interested in Dillon, he would "shear off" and freeze her out, or he would subject her to one of his lectures about the inferiority of the female brain—that was sure to scare her away. In his autobiography, Dillon says that it was all a matter of ethics; for the girl's sake, he had to protect her from his own advances. It would not be right to raise her expectations of marriage, since he could not father children. A healthy young woman should not be allowed to fall in love with a sterile man— she would only end up heartbroken.

In fact, Dillon was terrified. Now a virgin in his midthirties, he was equipped with a semierect, mostly numb sexual organ that resembled a small party balloon. Were he to declare his love to a woman, he would have to swear her to secrecy, confess his whole embarrassing history, then follow that up with a science lesson to explain all the unusual features of his body. After he'd bared himself to her, she would give him *that look*, the one that showed she no longer believed in his manhood. So it was hardly worth the bother. Furthermore, what if she betrayed his confidence? What if she told her friends? Within days, all his classmates at Trinity would know, and then, of course, the tabloids.

He was terrified the reporters would descend on him at any moment, flashbulbs popping, pencils scrawling, questions flying. As a member of the British aristocracy who had not only changed sex but also submitted himself to a science-fiction surgery, he knew he was a tabloid story waiting to happen. He suffered nightmares in which he woke up back in the garage, still a half-man, half-woman—nightmares in which the past few years had never happened. And those bad dreams sprang from an awful truth, the one drawback of his new and treasured freedom. His status as an ordinary man was conditional. It depended on silence and subterfuge. It could all be destroyed by one stray rumor.

For now, of course, he was safe. Just about everyone he knew thought of him as a born man, an ordinary fellow; all of Dillon's mental energies went into keeping it that way. His secret festered inside him, as secrets do when there's no one to share them. Dillon, who thought of himself as a scrupulously honest person, now lied to many of the people he knew—little lies, unimportant lies, but still they ate away at him. For instance, to gain admittance to the Trinity rowing team, he claimed that he'd won a prize for the Brasenose men's team at Oxford; he could not say what prizes he'd actually won nor reveal the name of the team to which he had actually belonged. He loved his chums on the rowing crew enough to put the group photo on his mantel; yet he'd had to deceive them all.

Late in his medical-school career, to obscure any lingering resemblance to Laura on his face, he grew the trim little goatee in the style of King George VI. After that, he felt safe enough to drop into Folkestone, and the aunts welcomed him back—now it seemed unlikely that a neighbor would recognize him as Laura.

Aside from family and a few old friends, Dillon could only be truthful with one other group of people: his readers. In 1946, William Heinemann Medical Books published a small run of *Self: A Study in Ethics and Endocrinology*. The title suggested a work on medical ethics; and indeed, the first two chapters drone on and on, lecturing about hormones. Only in the third chapter does Dillon begin the *real* book. In that hidden manifesto Dillon pleaded on behalf of transsexuals, describing to readers the awful loneliness of the condition. He even hazarded to tell a story very like his own: "The girl," he writes, describing the transsexual type, "[is] lean and wiry, scorns dolls and girls' games, likes to play Indians and soldiers, and is ever ready for some risky adventure or a fight . . . Yet [she will] menstruate normally."[17]

It seems incredible that Dillon, so terrified of publicity, would publish a book under his own name that declared his sympathy for

The cover of Michael Dillon's first book, published in 1946.

transsexuals, argued for sex-change operations (which almost no one at the time understood were possible), and insisted the British government should subsidize hormone treatments.

Yet he did. He sent his message out dressed up in a respectable cover and padded with a lecture about endocrinology—it was a scandalous book in drag as a boring one. The risk he took speaks to his loneliness. He knew so few fellow sufferers, so few who could understand. Dillon no doubt prayed that a troubled young man or woman would find the book, read it furtively, and then contact him—thus could he create a community of people like himself.

This is the response he got to his book: several letters from homosexual men. One of them demanded that Dillon supply him with a list of all the gay men in London. He had risked exposure, and for what? It seemed now he would always be alone.

CHAPTER 6
ORCHID

ROBERT COWELL STILL RACED CARS ON THE WEEKEND, but the problem of speed—how to squeeze as much as possible out of an engine—no longer interested him. In his mind, he had already begun living as a woman, and a woman could not, in the late 1940s, call herself an engineer.

And so Cowell switched to haute couture, paying dearly to learn the business of dress design. Once again, he borrowed money from his parents; he put up four thousand pounds to become a stakeholder in Sheridan of London Designs, which made gowns for films and celebrities. His investment in the company allowed him to become the firm's director, at least in name, and more important, to apprentice with a top designer, who was supposed to teach him her trade. It was a financially ruinous move, given that Cowell had already lost thousands of pounds on his last venture. But right now, money was the least of his problems.

He could no longer exist as a man, and yet he remained a man. The dress shop became his only refuge. There, he was learning a whole new language that he was making his own, the language of women: *peplum, raglan, dart, toile, placket, seersucker, seam* and *hem*, and *oh, darling, you look ravishing.* Cowell lurked in the back of the shop, out of sight of the women who came in for fittings, soaking it all up.

With the new job, he found he had no choice but to move to a more bohemian neighborhood, where a man could introduce himself as a would-be fashion designer without getting spit on. He circulated in what he called the artist clubs—*artist* had become Cowell's favorite euphemism for homosexuals, whom he disdained. He found them so disagreeable that he could not even bear to use the word *homosexual*. He called them "pansies" or "artists" or "gentlemen of no particular sex." And now, what he'd most feared had happened: he lived among them, and everyone assumed that he was one.

He needed to be able to pass as a woman, and fast, to escape this predicament. By this time, Cowell had found an endocrinologist who had agreed to help him. Estrogen—he was taking regular doses—worked miraculous changes on his body. "Almost overnight I acquired an unusually good complexion," and his sinewy arms slimmed down. Before the hormones he "had been able to hold out a service rifle in each hand, at arm's length and parallel to the ground, without letting either rifle drop."[1] After hormones, the muscles in his wrists became so delicate that he had to hide them under his sleeves when he went out in his man's coat. His chest and face hair thinned; the hair on his head thickened. And suddenly, he craved chocolate with such ferocity that he could go through boxes of bonbons.

As Cowell tells it, she decided to switch sex because "I had no desire to become a freak."[2] But for more than two years, Cowell would remain locked in a male name and legal identity. She was confined to trousers—except in the privacy of her apartment or her artistic neighborhood. For a time, her transformation would make her odd indeed, an in-between person who could pass for neither male or female. But she endured this ugly-duckling period because her endocrinologist had given her hope. She had, as yet, no surgeon willing to help her complete her transition; nor had she found a doctor who would sign a letter that would allow her to change her birth certificate. But she began to believe that she might someday become a woman.

For now she dressed in men's suits, generously cut to hide her developing breasts and hips. Still, people gawked. She suffered a hazing remarkably similar to Dillon's during his in-between period. "I preferred to steer clear of children and elderly ladies," who could be cruelly candid, she wrote.[3] One night in a restaurant, Cowell— who had done her best to disguise herself as a male, with a short haircut, a double-breasted blazer, and blue tie—realized that she couldn't pass as a man at all anymore. "It was obvious that nearly everyone in the room was arguing about my sex."[4] After that, Cowell sat in dark corners or avoided restaurants altogether.

She estimated that about half the strangers she spoke to during those days would "go out of their way to treat me as though I were an unpleasant, perverted freak. They had no hesitation in making their attitude abundantly clear, perhaps because they considered that I had no feelings at all, perhaps because they wanted to hurt me as much as possible."[5]

Unlike Cowell, Michael Dillon had encountered few legal hurdles when he wanted to change his sex—he'd been able to obtain both surgeries and the documents. But then, he had started out with a women's body, and there were few taboos against altering female genitals. An entire field of medicine—gynecology—devoted itself to the inspection, medicating, and sometimes removal of women's sexual organs. In England and the United States during Dillon's era, ovaries were understood to be in need of supervision by doctors— frail, prone to disease, painful, crazy-making. Therefore, the radical modification of women's bodies—even when that modification included reclassifying women as men—drew little attention. For instance, during the 1930s and '40s, a patient could walk into Harold Gillies's examining room as a legal female and walk out with the necessary papers to become a man—all within a few hours.

It was far more difficult for those who had been born with male bodies to switch. To change his legal sex, a man would need a note from a doctor testifying that he was in fact a female, and to obtain that document he would need the doctor to examine him and certify that he did not have testicles. And no doctor in Britain would consent to amputate testicles, because of the mayhem law, the centuries-old ban against cutting off the testicles (or any other healthy part) of a man who might become a soldier. That left people like Roberta Cowell in an impossible bind.

Even by the late 1950s and early 1960s, British surgeons refused to castrate men who wanted to become women. During those years, sex-change patients traveled to Holland or France to have their testicles amputated. That done, the patient might be able to have the rest of the surgeries performed in Britain, if she could find a sympathetic surgeon. "Castrated abroad," the British surgeon would scrawl into his notes—making it clear that he himself had not performed the shady operation.[6]

But in 1949, the "castrated abroad" option did not yet exist. So Cowell found herself stranded halfway to womanhood—unable to obtain either the legal documents or the operations she needed. She was terrified of being stuck that way for the rest of her life, neither Robert nor Roberta, a man-woman scuttling through "artistic" neighborhoods with a wig hidden in her briefcase.

Then she discovered a book that gave her hope: it was a slim medical volume wrapped in a cream-colored jacket. The author argued in favor of sex-change operations—not as a theoretical possibility, but as if the surgeries already existed. Cowell wrote to him through his publisher. She needed his advice. Would he see her?

He wrote back. He discouraged her from coming to Dublin where he lived; he did not want to meet with her before he knew about the nature of the problem. Then she sent another letter to him; this time she confessed that she'd gotten stuck between the sexes—and begged for his help. In the end, he set up a lunch with her in London.

And that's how their fateful meeting came about, that first restaurant date where it all began. Roberta Cowell perched across the table from him; she was packed into a business suit, her hair cropped short, her cheeks blushing in the heat of the close room, her easy laugh, her little jokes, the beautiful, manicured hands. She resembled—well—Laura Dillon, an awkward girl, still stuck in between, aristocratic yet ostracized, a refugee from her former life.

Roberta plied Dillon with questions: Who was the best surgeon for a sex change? Was it possible to reregister as a woman? Roberta needed him to act the man for her, to guide her, share the benefit of his experience.

Dillon trusted her immediately—more than that, he felt himself drawn in, caught by those dark eyes. By the end of lunch, Dillon had confessed his deepest secrets to her: how he'd lived as Laura, how he'd begun dosing himself with testosterone, and then how he'd found his way to Harold Gillies, who had changed his life.

On their first rendezvous, he'd swept in as her protector: in the beginning, he'd been the one in power, the one on top, the—well—man. But in a blink it switched. Now he was the one writing to her twice a day, foolishly scrawling notes in between his visits to patients. "No inhibitions are going to stop me saying, 'I love you.' I love you with the whole of me. *Te amo, ergo habebo te, Q.E.D.*' "[7] There it was, clear as a mathematical proof, the one true fact amid all the questions and doubts of his final year of medical school. He loved her. He would have her.

Although her side of that 1950–51 correspondence has not survived, it seems that, in the early months of their courtship, Cowell encouraged Dillon to believe she'd fallen in love, too. She presented him with glamorous photographs of herself in the blond wig, black eyes glaring at the camera, looking as bold as an American film star. He displayed a photo prominently in his flat and showed her off to visitors.

Michael Dillon escorts his aunt Daisy down a street in Folkestone, in 1950; it was the year he met Roberta. *From the collection of Liz Hodgkinson*

Then one day, he appeared in Folkestone with a flaming blonde on his arm. Dillon had been visiting his aunts ever since his beard had grown in, the clipped goatee that hid his former identity. Of course, Roberta was the ultimate beard—no chance anyone would recognize him as he emerged from the railroad station when he had Roberta laughing and tottering on her heels beside him. The aunts had approved of the charming, lively girl he brought home: she spoke with the right kind of accent and came from a family more famous than their own. She'd make an excellent wife.

Except, of course, for one great impediment that kept him from Roberta. He could not tell the aunts about it, nor the friends to whom he showed off her photograph. His fiancée had a penis and testicles.

Dillon could refer Roberta to Harold Gillies and a crew of other sympathetic doctors. But he could not give her what she wanted—a doctor to perform the castration. An orchidectomy, that was the proper name for the operation. Dillon loved to call things by their proper names. He liked to lecture his Bobbie about Latin words— for though she'd come from a prominent family, she'd never finished her schooling, and he felt the need to correct her. Orchidectomy. Sounds like *orchid*. Which makes one think of the scrotum as a pale tropical flower clinging to the dark notch of a body. She would not be able to get one in England, not for any amount of money. Surely Gillies couldn't help. Orchidectomy. The name of the surgery like the name of something beautiful and unobtainable, like the name of a perfume, entirely female.

And here's where the story gets exceedingly odd. A single document, one piece of paper, has survived to suggest that Michael Dillon was more than just Roberta Cowell's suitor. The document suggests that the besotted, head-over-heels, sexually innocent Michael Dillon risked everything for what he saw as his one shot at ordinary love.

The document reads as follows:

"I, R.C. have, of my own free will asked and persuaded L.M.D., who I am aware is an unqualified man, a 5th year medical student, to perform an orchidectomy upon me. I am also aware that his operating experience has been confined solely to assisting at operations as a resident pupil in hospital and to one appendectomy in the presence of a surgeon and that he has neither seen nor practiced this particular operation. I desire that he be absolved from all responsibility in this operation, due to possible hemorrhage or sepsis, which I am desirous to undergo being fully aware that either might, per fortunam, be fatal."[8]

The document is not dated, but must have been drawn up between the two in either 1950 or 1951, and indicates that Dillon would perform the operation on his own, outside of a hospital. He apparently insisted on some written agreement in order to protect himself in case Roberta bled to death during the operation. It's not clear how Dillon managed to obtain surgical tools or whether he used anesthesia.

I want to protect you, he told her in his letters. And now he had a chance to do just that, to be her hero, to save her, just as he had been saved.

Most important, the operation would allow him to marry Roberta. Once she was rid of those testicles, she could change her birth certificate. Then she'd be a legal woman; he was a legal man, and they could get on with their lives.

That is, if she lived.

She lived.

Dillon placed the amputated testicles in a jar of formaldehyde for further study. He may have done this at the behest of Sir Harold Gillies, who would later examine the sample; in Gillies's case study of Roberta Cowell, he suggests that he knew full well that Cowell had been castrated in England, in violation of the law. When Gillies studied the testicles many months later, he declared them atrophied—not surprising, since Cowell had been taking high doses of estrogen for two years. Because the testicles would not have been functional, Gillies argued that "had the castration been performed in Great Britain, the law of mayhem in reference to mutilation would not have applied."[9] The fact that Gillies dropped this sentence into his study of Cowell indicates that he knew exactly how and where she'd lost her testicles, and that he thought it necessary to protect Dillon and himself from prosecution under the law.

In March 1951, Dillon announced his engagement to Miss Cowell. The aunts were thrilled, as was Dillon's cousin Joan and his beloved tutor from Oxford, Jimmy McKie. An unexceptional life, the kind other people took for granted, dangled before Dillon. It was so close he could almost touch it—the plush chairs and the hush before Sunday dinner, a wife who brought him his pipe and enjoyed with him the sanctified sexual acts of marriage. Gillies had built him a penis just for this, had urged him to go out, find a girl, and marry her. Now he would.

It was the practical matters that consumed him: Where would they marry? What hymn should the organist play at the wedding? How would he ever manage to pass his medical-school exams? How would he raise the funds to support a woman like Roberta, with her taste for designer clothes and fast cars?

While he worked out the particulars, he sent her a package and told her to hide it in a drawer. She was not to open it until he passed his medical exams.

Roberta Cowell had her own exam to pass. She had made an appointment with Dr. George Dusseau, a gynecologist on Wimpole Street, where the posh doctors practiced behind genteel brick walls and brass plates. She had a plan: the doctor would examine her, discover she had no testicles, and would write up a note declaring her to be an intersexual, a person born with anomalous genitals. The note would allow her to change her birth certificate. That was the theory; Cowell was not at all sure that Dusseau would comply. "As

Roberta Cowell in the early 1950s. *The Hulton Archive*

my appointment drew near I became more and more jittery, and on the morning of the day I was to see the [doctor] I was in an advanced state of dither," Cowell wrote.[10] Her future depended on what he saw when he looked at her genitals—and what he saw might very well not look female.

He x-rayed her, prodded, squinted, palpated, and then left her in the room to dress. Cowell claims that she pressed her ear to the door and listened as the doctor discussed her case. "There is not the slightest doubt whatever. The patient is quite definitely not a man—she is undoubtedly a woman," the doctor said—or that's what she heard.[11] Cowell was a notoriously unreliable source when it came to the medical facts of her case.

Dusseau agreed to write the note for her.

On May 17, 1951, she became legally female.

Dillon called and called. No answer. He dropped by her flat in London, two tickets in his pocket, but she was not at home.

Roberta Cowell had a busy social life now. She still dressed as a man for work, but in her off-hours, she strutted down city streets in high heels, her corn-colored wig spilling over her shoulders, her skirt billowing around her calves.

Dillon was only one of her admirers.

In July 1951, Dillon found out he'd passed his medical exams. "It was too good to be true," he wrote. He had become "a respected member of the community." That night, he allowed himself to join his classmates in carousing: beer, gin, whiskey. The next day he kneeled in a church and thanked the Absolute, the Father-God, or "whatever it was" for his luck: he'd become a man, now a doctor, and soon a husband. It all far surpassed his fantasies of what might be possible. And then he wrote to Bobbie: Go ahead, open the package I sent you, look inside. I passed my exams and we can marry.

But his elation was short-lived. At the end of that summer, Dillon rode his bike away from the Royal City of Dublin hospital, weaving through the streets, still reeling from what he'd just learned. He had imagined himself to be enormously gifted, but his test scores had not borne out that theory: though he'd passed, he ranked at the low end of his class. Several female students ranked above him. There it was, incontrovertible evidence: He was not a brilliant medical mind after all, one of the star students who would be asked to stay on at the Dublin hospital, to be groomed for a plum position. Dillon had been so confident he'd be in the top of the class, and therefore stay on at the teaching hospital, that he hadn't bothered to look for a backup job. Now he had nothing. How on earth would he support his future wife?

And then came another blow, one so devastating that Michael Dillon never wrote about it at all. Bobbie turned him down.

They met and she explained her reasons. The details of that meeting between them have been lost; Cowell did not say how she broke the news except that she was firm. Always free with her opinions, she would likely have left Dillon with the impression that he was not man enough for her. Years later, she said she didn't really regard him as a real man at all: "As far as I was concerned, it would have been two females getting married, and I was certainly not interested in him in that kind of way."[12]

Now he'd have to remove her photograph from the mantel. He'd have to explain that he'd been jilted to the aunts, and to his old tutor Jimmy McKie, and to his acquaintances at medical school. But worse than that was knowing he'd risked everything for her, and she dropped him. If she ever let on how she'd come to be castrated, he would lose his license to practice medicine; worse, he'd become wrapped up in a scandal more humiliating than his own sex change.

Dillon never mentioned Roberta Cowell again.

CHAPTER 7
A PASSPORT INTO THE WORLD OF WOMEN

SOMETIME IN 1952, Harold Gillies cleared off a table in his consulting office, placing a bust of Rudolf Virchow, the father of modern pathology, off to the side. He lifted the torso of a male corpse onto the empty table. Then, smoking furiously, he began to practice for the next day's surgery on Roberta Cowell. Gillies slipped the sleeve of skin off the corpse's penis and discarded the contents of the organ, leaving a large flap of skin. Shaping that skin around one of his fingers, he formed it into an envelope that would fit into a cavity he had already cut in the torso's groin, creating a vagina. The trick appeared to work. Tomorrow, he would perform the first vaginal construction that had ever been attempted in Britain.[1] "This was the big one," according to Ralph Millard, the American surgeon who assisted Gillies.[2] Because there was almost no medical literature on male-to-female sex-change operations, Gillies would have to extemporize.

Of course, Roberta Cowell's anatomy did not exactly match that of the corpse's: she had already had her testicles removed. The American surgeon, Millard, confirmed this fact—when he examined Cowell, he says, it was obvious that her testicles had been surgically removed, though he did not know how or where that operation had occurred.[3]

While Gillies and Millard labored in a back room, doing a dry run of the surgery on a dead man, Roberta Cowell entered the clinic from the front. She checked in wearing a skirt and a blond wig. The nurses showed her to her room. She lay on the bed, tossing and turning, her heart pounding. "I was scared stiff. I was off on an unknown road to an unknown future . . . The operation might not succeed . . . I might be desperately uncomfortable afterwards; I might be in great pain. Perhaps the story would leak out, and life afterwards would be impossible."[4]

Two days later, she woke from a drugged haze. Her hands were swollen and covered with bruises from the anesthesia the doctors had pumped into her. Bandages hid the bottom half of her torso. When Gillies came in to remove the catheter, he announced that the operation had been a success: she had a vagina. After all her worries, it had been that easy. She recovered and checked out.

But soon, Cowell decided the vagina was not enough; to be truly female, she would need a new face. She could not bear to be stuck with Robert Cowell's profile—he had been another person entirely. He'd had a perfectly serviceable male nose, but it wouldn't do for a gamine. She went back to Gillies for a button nose, "slightly retroussé," as she put it.[5] Also, fuller lips. Cosmetic surgery on the face, in those days, remained a rarity. The ordinary girl still resigned herself to a wide nose or a birthmark. But Cowell was no ordinary girl. She emerged from Gillies's treatments with a turned-up, flirty little nose and a big film-star mouth that seemed to be made for scarlet lipstick.

Men swarmed as she tottered down the street on her high heels. They rubbernecked as she strutted past them. They slowed down in cars to ask her directions—and then wanted to go out to dinner with her. They bumped into her, then offered to buy her a drink by way of apology. Those with manners dashed up to her on the street and said, "Excuse me, I know it's very rude to speak to you, but isn't it a nice day?"[6]

She worked hard that first year at being a woman, learning to cook, to apply makeup, to strut on high heels, and to snatch a hand off her knee. It was as if, she wrote, "each new thing I learned [was] another visa stamped in the passport I needed for entry into the world of womankind."[7]

She had given up her passport into the world of men. That had cost her dearly—thousands upon thousands of pounds. In 1952, Cowell had to dissolve the company that she'd founded years before, in the hopes of designing an Aspin engine to showcase at the Grand Prix. Cowell did not dare risk calling attention to herself by competing in one of the world's top races. "The possibility of publicity came up and I voluntarily liquidated the [engine-design] company and lost all the money," she wrote. Cowell would never design a winning engine or race in a major event again.[8]

Michael Dillon had graduated from one of the best medical schools in Ireland, but in 1951 he accepted a yearlong residency that paid only one pound a week. For that small sum, Dillon would act as surgeon, specialist, and house doctor in a fifty-bed hospital in the north of Dublin.

With his modest inheritance, he might have waited for something better to come along. Still, this was the only job he'd managed to get right away, and Dillon was eager to keep himself busy and forget Roberta Cowell. He took the position. That year, in a frenzy of altruism, he organized teas and trips to the theater for his patients, founded a lending library inside the hospital, and raised money to install radios and headphones beside every bed so that patients could listen to music.

Dillon's charges stirred in him a new and powerful empathy, particularly an orphan boy named Johnny. The boy had arrived at the hospital at age fifteen; now, three years later, with his TB in remission, he was free to leave. When it came time to discharge Johnny, however, Dillon discovered the boy had only two possessions to his name: a ballpoint pen and a pair of shoes that he'd outgrown. Johnny did not even have a suit of street clothes to wear out the door. Or a place to go.

That night, after he'd discovered Johnny's predicament, Dillon returned to his little house and surveyed all his possessions: the silver rowing cups on the mantel, the leather chairs, the side table with whiskey set out on it, and the closet full of suits. His belongings—not particularly lavish, to be sure—struck him as obscene. "How could one own all these things when there was a boy with absolutely nothing?" he asked himself.[9] Dillon was so shaken by Johnny's poverty that he vowed to give up one tenth of his earnings to charity—a promise that he would keep, and then some.

In February 1953, Christine Jorgensen landed at Idlewild Airport (now JFK Airport) after enduring a series of treatments in Copenhagen that had transformed her from a skinny, jug-eared boy into a blond debutante with a grin of pearls at her neck. Gathering her fur coat, Jorgensen ducked through the door of the plane and was confronted with the evidence of her fame. Three hundred reporters fought to get closer, yelling at her, popping flashbulbs. "Where did you get the fur coat?" "How about a cheesecake shot, Christine?" "Do you expect to marry?"[10]

And so, Christine Jorgensen became known as the "first" transsexual—though she was certainly not the first to go through a sex-change operation or to use hormones to transform her body.

"I clutched my belongings more closely to me," she wrote about that moment when she surveyed the reporters below her. "[I] stumbled slightly as I reached out to grasp a handrail, and started slowly down the landing stairs . . . At that moment, I was descending into a new and alien world."[11]

That year, she would become the number one news story in America. EX-GI BECOMES BLONDE BEAUTY. MDS RULE CHRIS 100 PERCENT WOMAN. DISILLUSIONED CHRISTINE TO BECOME MAN AGAIN!! I'VE FALLEN IN LOVE WITH CHRISTINE, SAYS REPORTER. The tabloids found dozens of ways to re-spin her story. Jorgensen, with her considerable charm and wit, managed to rise above the attacks and sneers and became a sort of ambassador from the land of transsexuals, a place she portrayed as being as modern and spick-and-span as Copenhagen itself. "I knew that much of the curiosity and interest stemmed from the understandable fact that people were looking for answers," she wrote.[12] Jorgensen did her best to supply those answers, plowing through the twenty thousand letters written to her and helping those she could. At the time, she was so much a phenomenon that even envelopes addressed to "Christine Jorgensen, USA" reached her.

Tabloid magazines would accuse her of fakery—they insisted she must be a woman who pretended to have a sex change, because no man could effect such a miraculous transformation. Others portrayed her as a pervert and a freak. Jorgensen countered with her own public appearances; dressed in designer gowns, she deployed a hostessy charm that put everyone at ease. The Scandinavian Society named her woman of the year. She lunched with Danny Kaye, Milton Berle, and Truman Capote. Always, she showed up with her ice-colored hair perfectly coiffed, skin glowing, lips plump and red.

Natural-born females took note. If hormones and surgery could make a biological man look that good, what might the treatments do for women? The estrogen therapy that she'd been using for years, Jorgensen claimed, had given her skin an ethereal softness and filled her with a sense of well-being. And unlike the surgical component of Jorgensen's transformation, hormones were easy to obtain. Anyone who was determined enough could find a way to buy estrogen from a drugstore. In fact Jorgensen had done just that.

In 1948, a college boy named George Jorgensen worked up the nerve to consult a top endocrinologist in Connecticut. "I came here to ask you what I can do about my feelings of being a sexual mix-up," the young man stammered. "Is it at all possible that the trouble lies in a glandular or chemical imbalance of some kind?"

The doctor refused to help; he also committed the further cruelty of keeping Jorgensen in the dark about estrogen, which was then a readily available drug. Instead, he sent Jorgensen off to a psychiatrist, and that was the end of it.

Except it wasn't. Jorgensen stumbled across Paul de Kruif's then best seller about testosterone, *The Male Hormone*. He read it so many times the binding split, memorizing passages about estradiol (a variant of estrogen). Jorgensen had never heard of anyone using hormones to change sex, but he decided to see if it was possible. He wandered into a section of New Haven where he knew no one would recognize him, found a drugstore, and asked for estradiol.

"That's a pretty strong chemical," the man behind the counter warned. "We're not supposed to sell it without a prescription."

Jorgensen claimed to be a medical student working on a hormone experiment and walked away with a hundred tablets.[13]

After months on the pill, he began to look more androgynous, with luscious skin and small breasts, though strangers still "read" him as a boy or man. What he loved most about the pill was the way it transformed his mind and mood: it erased a sense of numbness, a fatigue, and "disturbing thoughts" that had plagued him all through his life. Estrogen had worked on his mind, he felt, in the same way it had transformed his skin: turning it plush and pink, smoothing out the blemishes. A few years later, he would disappear to Copenhagen, where he received further hormone treatments and surgery, returning to the United States as Christine Jorgensen—a living advertisement for the magic of technology.

Jorgensen offered a model not just for transsexuals, but also for women who longed for bigger busts and that creamy, dreamy skin. In 1953, Jorgensen's friend Gen Angelo threw a charity bridge party where Christine became the star attraction in the roomful of women. "I was bombarded with questions right and left, people wondering why she did it, asking if her hair was naturally blonde and how she got her beautiful complexion," Angelo wrote. Several women began "asking for hormone treatments to give them the same smooth complexion."[14] Jorgensen's décolletage—that beautiful swell of cleavage just visible between the satin folds of her gown—would no doubt have inspired wonder, too. Breast-augmentation surgery was still rare.

In the 1950s, new technologies existed that could radically transform appearance, but these technologies were being used to their fullest effect only by a few people. Those people were transsexuals. When Christine Jorgensen stepped out of that plane in 1953, she showed America how very thin the line between male and female could be. She also announced a new age was coming. An age in which the body—any body—could be molded into the shape that the mind demanded.

Roberta Cowell's phone rang in the middle of the night. On the other end of the line, one of her boyfriends, a newspaper reporter, gushed about an incredible story he'd just heard. An American named George Jorgensen had flown to Denmark, where doctors had transformed him into a woman. Cowell's boyfriend was sure that the story must be a hoax. How could a man turn into a woman?

Cowell found it amusing that her boyfriend was so shocked by Christine. What would the newspaperman have done if he'd known he was dating a transsexual? "Poor man, he'd have a fit!" Cowell quipped.[15]

With Christine Jorgensen in the spotlight, it didn't take long for the tabloids to catch on to Cowell. In early 1954, she learned that her story was about to blow up in the British press. It's not clear who had tattled on her. Cowell herself may have been the one who leaked it. By the spring of 1954, she had negotiated with the *Picture Post* magazine to write up her confessions; she sold her story for twenty thousand pounds—what amounted to a small fortune in the 1950s—according to a rival tabloid, the *Pictorial*.[16]

Cowell needed that money badly. She owed thousands of pounds after the collapse of her engine-design firm; the *Picture Post* deal would help her pay off her debt and start over again. And, of course, publishing her autobiography in the tabloids would allow her to tell her version of the story first. By that time, Cowell did have her own version.

She insisted that even though Robert Cowell had fathered two children and passed his RAF physical, he had always possessed, in addition to the usual male equipment, a set of dormant ovaries hidden in his belly. The trauma of prisoner-of-war camp, she claimed, had set the ovaries into action, pumping out estrogen into Robert Cowell's body; that's why small breasts had spontaneously sprouted on his chest.

As Cowell told it, she'd never really had a sex change at all because she'd been born a hermaphrodite, a person whose body exhibited characteristics of both sexes. She'd resorted to surgery and hormones so that she would not have to live as a two-sexed person. Wasn't that a reasonable enough desire?

"After the sex change, her life was wholly dedicated to preserving the myth that she was 'really' female and had been all along," according to journalist Liz Hodgkinson. "The effort of preserving this falsehood eventually, I believe, unhinged her."[17]

In the last forty years, the sex-change autobiography has become a genre unto itself. Dozens of transsexuals have written up their stories, and many of these bildungsromans, with their before-and-after story lines, have become classics, most especially Jan Morris's masterfully written *Conundrum*.

But when Roberta Cowell sat down at the typewriter to bang out her own book, she had only one model to draw on. Cowell's autobiography—serialized in the *Picture Post* magazine and then later released as a potboiler titled *Roberta Cowell's Story*—would be the first full-length sex-change memoir ever written in the English language. It would be only the second such book ever published in the world—the first had been Lili Elbe's story, which had appeared in 1932 as *Ein Mensch wechselt sein Geschlecht* and was translated into English a year later (as *Man into Woman*).

In the late 1920s, Lili Elbe had whirled through the parties and cafés of Paris, a middle-aged flapper with eyes hidden under the shadow of her sun hat, and a secret behind her demure smile. Lili had been born a man. She had resorted to every treatment she could find to make herself feminine. More specifically, she wanted to turn back the clock, so she could become a *young* woman. Since she lived in the era of organology, monkey-gland treatments, and X-ray miracle cures, doctors were only too eager to tease her with the possibility of such a transformation. Today, Lili is regarded as the first person to have survived a sex-change operation. But that is not how Lili herself would have described her medical odyssey. Instead, Lili regarded herself as a person who had been "rejuvenated," restored to the youth and femininity that were hallmarks of her true self.

Lili began as an artist named Einar Wegener in the early 1900s in a studio with a sweeping view of Copenhagen. Einar's wife—then a painter of some fame—had needed a female model to finish up one of her portraits. She'd pleaded with Einar to dress in drag, sit before her, and model. He had such nice legs, after all. Neither of them expected what happened next: in his wig and dress, he metamorphosed into an adorable gamine. They named her Lili. After Einar pulled on his trousers again, she vanished—but her presence still thrummed between them.

For years, Lili remained a kind of party game or performance-art piece; when life turned a little dull, Einar's wife would coax Lili out for the evening to accompany her to balls and picnics and cafés. The next morning Lili would disappear, dissolving back into Einar Wegener again.

For one entire year while the couple traveled, they more or less forgot about Lili. But then, when Gerda, Einar's wife, settled down to work again, frowning at the easel in concentration, she found she couldn't do without the French girl. Lili had become her muse. So once again, they summoned her, that laughing sprite who gamboled around the studio. A series of portraits resulted: Lili peered out of canvas after canvas, pouting in furs, her face as iconic and sphinxlike as any art deco beauty's. For over a decade, Lili lived that way, in fits and starts, mostly on the wall, her face frozen. And then sometime in the 1920s, the game turned desperately serious. Einar Wegener felt his own self slipping away and Lili's taking over.

Stuck in a middle-aged male body, Wegener wrote, "I seemed to myself like a deceiver, like a usurper who reigned over a body which had ceased to be his, like a person who owned merely the façade of his house."[18] Another, truer self lived inside him—the French girl. For her to come to life, Wegener would have to cross two lines: he would have to reverse both his age and his sex.

He traipsed from doctor to doctor seeking a cure: could they do anything to extinguish him and bring Lili into being? Doctors who examined Wegener described his body as that of an ordinary male— not so well endowed perhaps, but ordinary. Still with no concept of transsexuality to draw on, the top medical men of the day decided that Wegener's urges must come from *somewhere* inside the body. So they agreed he must have ovaries hidden under his flat belly.

Doctors did not have much to offer Wegener besides the hope that he might have been a woman all along—the first doctor he saw suggested that ovaries had been lurking inside Wegener ever since he was born; they were damaged or perhaps stunted organs, not strong enough to pump out the hormones that would make his body look both female and young. Wegener's doctor had not actually *seen* the ovaries, but he zapped the patient's belly with X-rays anyway, to "stimulate" them.

The treatment did no good. It's likely, of course, that Wegener had no ovaries at all—that his femaleness could not be located in his abdomen, nor anywhere in the flesh. But the doctors of the time—and Wegener himself—thought the personality of Lili must have sprung out of ovarian tissue. In the 1920s, the idea that maleness or femaleness could originate in our brains—rather than our genitals—would not have occurred to any doctor. Even Hirschfeld, the Berlin sexologist who was so ahead of his time, believed that the urge to cross-dress must have something to do with the glands. Since Einar Wegener felt he was turning into a young woman, his doctors believed that ovaries—hidden somewhere inside his body—must be creating his urges.

After X-rays failed to help, Wegener consulted with one of the top German gynecologists of the day. The doctor said exactly what Wegener wanted to hear: the withered, damaged ovaries could be replaced with new ones from a vibrant young woman. A pair of healthy ovaries, the gynecologist confirmed, would turn Wegener into Lili, once and for all.

At that time, human ovaries could be bought on the black market; a few daring older women, desperately seeking rejuvenation, had already put themselves under the knife, swapping old ovaries for new ones.[19] In the era before estrogen became available as a drug, doctors knew no other way to manipulate the hormone levels in a woman's body. Unfortunately, the operation was far more likely to kill the patient than to revivify her. Surgeons simply did not have the skills to transplant ovaries and keep them working—so the organs Einar Wegener received would be so much ornamentation.

Before the patient could receive his ovaries, however, he would have to undergo another experimental procedure. A team of doctors would transform his penis into a vagina. After a preliminary operation in which he endured a castration, Einar Wegener—now going by the name Lili—checked into a women's clinic in Dresden, to be cared for by gynecological specialists.

For weeks, Lili recovered from her castration and waited for a new pair of ovaries—exactly how the doctors obtained those ovaries, Lili does not say. The day finally came when a nurse assured Lili that the surgeon would operate on her imminently. The ovaries had been extracted from a twenty-seven-year-old woman, the nurse said, and would pump fluids into Lili's body that would make her young again.[20]

The operation was a success—in that Lili lived through it. After a long recuperation, she was finally able to check out of the women's clinic; in her purse, she carried a Danish passport that declared her to be a woman—the doctors had arranged that as well. Gerda helped her to the train, and they rode side by side to Berlin: girlfriends now, sisters, best friends. All traces of Einar Wegener—aside from the paintings he'd left behind—had vanished. He was as good as dead. In fact, Lili resented any associations between herself and the parasite who had once inhabited her body. She claimed not to even share his memories. "Lili stood in front of the old house of her parents; she remembered it remotely and hazily, like something of which one had dreamed. Her brother frequently asked her if she could remember this or that incident from [their] common childhood." She could not.[21]

As Lili Elbe saw it, she had not changed her sex; she had had to kill off Einar to become her true self. He had been a man in his forties with an established reputation as an artist and a soulful connection to his wife; Lili, on the other hand, was a young woman, newly liberated to roam the world, struggling to find a career, eager for her first romance. While Einer had been a few years older than Gerda, Lili declared herself to be far younger, a kind of "grown-up daughter."[22] She believed that she should be allowed to change the age, as well as the sex, listed on her passport: "I find it unjust for me to retain [Einar's] age and birthday, for my biological age is quite different from his . . . [He] and I have really nothing whatever to do with each other," she wrote.[23]

Lili Elbe claimed that surgery had allowed her to overcome her

Einar Wegener endured a series of groundbreaking surgeries, including the implantation of ovaries, to live as a woman. Afterward, he became Lili Elbe. *The Kinsey Institute for Research in Sex, Gender and Reproduction*

body entirely: to shatter the barriers of age and sex. So why shouldn't she become a mother, too? Doctors promised her a birth canal, a uterus. Lili endured another grueling operation to achieve the final and most irrefutable proof of femininity, and in its aftermath, in 1931, she died.

Unlike modern transgendered people, she had not been able to benefit from hormone therapy, since her transplanted ovaries were useless. But she did endure one of the first surgeries, perhaps *the* first, to reshape a penis into a vagina. This has made her a pioneer. Now, because scholars see her as the first sex-change patient, they tend to leave out the rest of the story: as much as Lili wanted to be female, she also wanted to be young.

While she was still transitioning, Roberta Cowell discovered a dusty, dog-eared volume of *Man into Woman*; Lili's story, never well known outside of Denmark, had long since been forgotten, an artifact from a more primitive medical era. Still, even though the scientific facts in the book were out-of-date, Cowell modeled her story on Einar/Lili's. She insisted she'd always had ovaries. That meant she was not an artificial woman but a *real* one.

The ovaries—imaginary or not—meant everything to her. "Once I realized that my femininity had a *physical* basis I did not despise myself so much."[24] Cowell claims that a doctor discovered the ovaries—though later, she could never produce this physician nor any proof of his diagnosis. She believed she had *always* been female, and the estrogen treatments and plastic surgery had only helped her achieve her true biological sex.

She released a statement along these lines to the press on March 6, 1954. Almost every major British paper, aside from the London *Times*, ran a story about Cowell that week, most of them on page one—these stories echoed her press release, repeating her fantastical

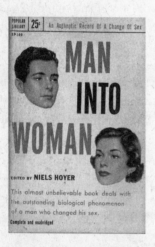

In 1952, Christine Jorgensen's sex change became a top story in U.S. newspapers. The following year, the Popular Library reissued Lili Elbe's biography from the 1930s; the publisher packaged the book in such a way that the long-ago story appeared to be breaking news. When Roberta Cowell sat down to write her own autobiography, she collected some of her outdated medical information from Lili Elbe's account.

claims.[25] In the United States, *Newsweek* cribbed from Cowell's press release: "In 1948 . . . [Robert Cowell's] mental outlook changed and his body showed female characteristics. On doctor's advice, Bob was treated with hormones to hasten the change." Roberta Cowell, the magazine reported, was now enjoying herself "somewhere in France."[26]

Indeed, as *Picture Post* released the first installment of her story, Cowell was hiding out in Europe, prepared for the horde of journalists who would descend upon her. They chased her to Italy, a noisy, flash-popping gaggle of them. The mob staked out the villa where she'd put herself into seclusion: Cowell wouldn't talk. The *Picture Post* had paid for her exclusive story, which ran in seven installments, and she had nothing more to add.

Failing to get any quotes out of Cowell, reporters scoured London for anyone who would tattle on her. They hung around pubs, hoping to get a word with Cowell's old mates from race-car-driving days. They interviewed plastic surgeons and endocrinologists, anyone

Roberta Cowell, fleeing from the paparazzi, stops to do some sightseeing in Italy. The photographer titled this image "Different Leanings." *The Hulton Archive*

who might have *anything* to say about sex changes, to feed the public's curiosity about Cowell. She was, after all, the first Brit known to have had a sex change, and the first to come along after the Christine Jorgensen frenzy.

Soon, with so many journalists tracking leads, Cowell's version of the story began to crumble. The *Pictorial* led the pack. It quoted Dr. George Dusseau, who'd signed the note that allowed Cowell to change her birth certificate. With that letter, he had not meant "to prove that Cowell had become physiologically a complete female. It was rather in the nature of a working certificate to enable the plastic surgeons to carry out their operations."[27] In other words, Dusseau had done his best to put Cowell into an entirely new legal category, one so new that it didn't yet have a name. She was a man, yes, but a man who *intended* to transform into a woman.

Rather than a miracle of nature, the article theorized, Cowell must have been a "transvestist—a man who is compelled by an overwhelming impulse to act as a woman and feels driven to stop at nothing to bring about and encourage all possible necessary changes." The *Pictorial* asserted that Roberta Cowell was no woman at all—only a man who'd used surgery as a form of cross-dressing. Soon, the *Pictorial* dropped another shocker. Cowell's father—a prominent surgeon—confirmed that Roberta was a "transvestist." She had not been born with ovaries, according to Sir Ernest Cowell, who had, of course, examined the son when he was an infant and confirmed he was a healthy male.[28]

By April, one tabloid had demoted Cowell from a transvestite into a monster. "There was no physical change that called for the operations," according to an article in *Sunday People*. "They were done purely to meet Cowell's abnormal craving. When all this [surgical] work was complete the horror that was Robert Cowell released himself on the world as 'Roberta.'" Cowell had become a Godzilla of false femininity, a threat to the moral core of the British nation. *Sunday People* demanded that Cowell's birth certificate be changed back again.

When another tabloid published a photo of Roberta Cowell arching one of her shapely legs as she gave her stocking a tug, *Sunday People* exploded in fury: "Could there be anything more revolting than this person pretending he is a 'glamour girl' when in fact he is merely a man who has been emasculinated [*sic*] and who has none of the vital feminine organs? . . . Cowell should face the fact that he is now nothing but an unhappy freak."[29]

For a month and a half, the British tabloids gossiped furiously about Cowell. And then the frenzy burned out. Incredibly, none of the newspapers had raised questions about how Cowell had managed to obtain a castration.

One of the few people in a position to tell her secret had put himself far beyond the reach of journalists, on a ship chugging across a wide emptiness of ocean, making its way toward the holy city of Jedda. Michael Dillon was bound for Mecca.

PART II
FIT THE MIND

CHAPTER 8
THE THIRD EYE

I N 1952, DILLON HAD SIGNED UP FOR A TOUR as a doctor on a merchant-navy ship sailing across the Red Sea. He regarded the job as a lark, a year of jaunting around the world before he started to look for a *real* job doing laboratory research. But that first day on a Pacific & Orient cargo ship, as soon as he'd settled into his cabin and slipped into his uniform, Dillon knew he belonged here. He fell in love with the decorated and gold-braided man he saw in the full-length mirror. As a small child, the first thing that Laura had ever really wanted had been a ship pilot's jacket and a cap (H.M.S. RENOWN) to go with it. Now, the impossible had happened: Dillon looked like the man Laura had dreamed of being.

True, he still had a long way to go. He had yet to lose his virginity. He was baffled by women. His brother refused to be seen with him. And though he'd worked himself into exhaustion over the past years, he had not become a medical genius like his hero Gillies. Still, the three stripes on his shoulder helped to make up for all of the disappointments. "I gazed with disbelief after adorning myself in my new plumes. Could this really be me? What a long way I had come from those garage days . . . I put on the [ship officer's] cap with its white cover and looked again." At dinner, his fellow officers welcomed him with backslaps and bonhomie, treating him as a member of their coterie. "I went to my bunk that night feeling intensely happy. This was the life for me!"[1]

The next year passed in a blur of blue water and shipboard dinners, seasick passengers and cocktails with the captain. By the end of
his first contract with the merchant navy, Dillon had fully grown
into his uniform; handsome and deeply tanned, he was seasoned
enough as a ship's doctor to improvise with medicines he picked up
in foreign ports and adventurous enough to ride a rickety bicycle
down a dirt road in Kenya.

Although he remained socially awkward—the years of being
jeered at had taken their toll—he did learn how to muddle through
most social situations. He smiled and let the three stripes on his
shoulder do most of the talking for him. Mostly, he kept to himself.

You could find *Burke's Peerage* and *Debrett's Peerage*—the two best-
known encyclopedias of the well-born—on the shelves of university libraries and in the reading rooms of certain British families.
They were fat, leatherbound tomes tooled with gold filigree that
listed the pedigrees of royals, dukes, viscounts, earls, and barons. In
both books, the Dillon family commanded the better part of a page.
In *Debrett's*, for instance, Dillon's brother, Bobby, appeared much
puffed up in print as Robert William Charlier Dillon, the eighth
baronet of Lismullen, a baron of the Holy Roman Empire. Alongside his name, a coat of arms frothed with decorations: a lion, several six-pointed stars, a falcon, a knight's helmet, and some swishy
organic matter that resembled arugula. First motto of the Dillon
family: "Whilst I breathe I hope." Backup motto: "Help from on
high." Underneath all of this heraldry, a small entry read, "Sister
living: Laura Maude."

In both *Debrett's Peerage* and *Burke's Peerage*, Laura Dillon continued
her weary existence. Dillon had managed to expunge the name
Laura from every other document, but he had yet to attempt to
change the listing in the peerage books.

About a decade earlier, Bobby had commanded that his sister,

Laura, must *never* clamor for recognition as part of the family, must *never* even show her face at the family estate. If Michael Dillon changed himself from *sister living* to *brother living* in the peerage books, he would break every one of Bobby's rules and then some. A *sister living* was an aristocratic nonentity—females inherited neither title nor property. But a *brother living* was an entirely different matter. Bobby and his wife had not produced any heirs, and it looked as if they never would, so if Michael Dillon changed his listing, he would put himself in line to become the ninth baronet of Lismullen.

By 1953, after a year of traveling the world and wearing an officer's uniform, Dillon had become so confident, so *entitled*, that he no longer felt he had to bow to Bobby's rules. When the ship docked in London, Dillon looked up the editor in charge of *Debrett's Peerage*, showed his birth certificate, and explained the delicate matter. It must have been an awkward conversation for the two men, but the editor, C. F. Hankinson, proved to be sympathetic; indeed, he agreed not only to correct the entry, but also to back Dillon as the next baronet if Bobby died first. Once the change appeared in *Debrett's*, the editor said, *Burke's Peerage* would follow suit.

By changing his listing in such august record books—by putting himself in line for the title of baronet—Dillon was taking an enormous risk of drawing attention to himself. Still, he felt safe. For years he'd passed as a born man, and no one had found him out; the tabloids no longer frightened him the way they once had.

And then the Roberta Cowell story broke. Dillon does not, of course, allude to the Cowell media blitz in his memoir. So it's hard to know what went through his mind when Roberta Cowell became a tabloid star in March of 1954. For a few weeks, she gazed from every newsstand, one hand on her cheek, fixing the camera with a smoldering stare. And when the book *Roberta Cowell's Story* appeared months later, Dillon must have been horrified to find that he was in it. Cowell dished an anecdote about meeting the author of a "book on ethics"; she described the author as a bearded man addicted to his pipe; she told how, at an intimate lunch, the author had confessed that he'd been born a "perfectly normal girl" and had had a sex change. She did not name him, but Roberta Cowell peppered her story with just enough clues that a perspicacious journalist might someday guess the rest.

Bobbie had betrayed him yet again.

Dillon's behavior suggests he may have been shaken up by the Cowell revelations—enough so that he decided to flee England. Up to that point, he had only committed to shipboard work for short periods. But in 1954, he signed a four-year contract with a ship that would ferry Muslim pilgrims to Mecca. The ship would chug around in giant loops between Singapore and Saudi Arabia and back again, picking up hajjists throughout Asia and delivering them to Jedda. Dillon would work among passengers and crew who did not speak English. At times the ship would teem with people; at other times, it would sail empty. Dillon would go weeks without seeing an English newspaper or one of his countrymen; if Roberta Cowell were to reveal his secret, the tabloids would find it nearly impossible to track him down.

Before he left on his first trip to Mecca, Dillon wandered along Charing Cross Road and bought armfuls of books by and about G. I. Gurdjieff, a mystic then popular among beatniks and intellectuals. Dillon had first become entranced by Gurdjieff's ideas a few years before, during his residency at the hospital in Dublin, just after Roberta Cowell had discarded him. Now, with years of empty time stretching ahead of him, Dillon planned to study Gurdjieff's system of self-improvement; the dead Greek-Armenian mystic would be his teacher, and Dillon would burn himself into a new shape, into someone harder and wiser, and far less capable of being hurt. He would begin "the Work." (Gurdjieff followers capitalized certain words to make them seem more profound; "doing the Work" meant following a program of self-examination and self-improvement.) Dillon—who had been reading philosophy and theology books ever since his breasts had swelled at age fifteen, who had endured a changeable and alien body, who ached for some kind of certainty—now decided that he would embark on a Search for Truth, capital S, capital T. After the ship set sail, he devoured Gurdjieff's books and those by the disciples P. D. Ouspensky and Maurice Nicoll; in his own memoir, Dillon quotes extensively from these texts, underlining the excerpts with thick black lines, as if he's haranguing his reader through his typewriter. " 'We cannot change the events but only our way of taking them—we cannot reform the world, we can only reform ourselves.' " And: "It is astonishing and terrifying that one can go on for years living with a false picture of oneself."[2]

The ideas were simple, really, so simple they would later be regurgitated in countless self-help books: You are the source of your misery. Therefore, rather than blaming your suffering on the conditions of your life, you must struggle to retrain yourself to get rid of bad habits. Gurdjieff's system promised a way to amputate personality defects—defensiveness, pigheadedness, greediness—and to create a better self. Dillon launched into this new program of refurbishment with the same determination that he'd once used to resculpt his chest and his genitals.

And for this transformation, too, he would have to depend on the help of other people, to put himself on the operating table, so to speak. "If we want to know how we look in a new suit . . . almost certainly, we go along and ask someone else how we look in it," Dillon wrote. The same is true for our personality—only other people can judge how it fits us, he conjectured. "If someone tells us some act or emotion of ours is ugly or does not become us, at once we are angry and try to . . . comfort ourselves with renewed assurances that all we are is perfect," Dillon wrote, noting that such denial was pointless. "I made a resolve never to defend myself against such criticisms again."[3] And so Dillon began the Work. It sounded easy enough in theory: he would invite criticism from people around him, listen carefully to their comments about his personality flaws, discover his faults, make a list of those faults, and perfect himself piece by piece.

Carrying out the plan was another matter entirely. When his only friend on the hajj ship, the captain, asked Dillon to stop acting like a know-it-all, Dillon immediately agreed and vowed to change. But he quickly learned that habits are more powerful than good intentions. Even after he'd resolved to stop lecturing and start listening to other people, Dillon found he could not break his addiction to know-it-all-ism. He went right on preaching to the few English-speaking crewmembers about Gurdjieff's ideas.

He had managed to utterly refashion his body. But his mind, it turned out, was much more resistant to change.

In 1955 or 1956, on a furlough from his shipboard job, Dillon returned to Folkestone to tend to the aunts. He'd gathered from their letters that they'd declined, but he was unprepared for what he found. Toto's miserliness—her psychosis, really—had reduced the two old women to Dickensian poverty. He found the octogenarians huddled around their stove in threadbare robes, toes poking out of the holes in their shoes. Toto refused to burn more than one lump of coal at a time, and so the house was freezing. The women had enough money for thousands of lumps of coal; their inheritance had quietly been growing in a bank account over the years. But Toto refused to squeeze more than a few pennies out of her purse for necessities.

Dillon bought them both fur-trimmed slippers the morning after he arrived. And just as he expected, Toto wrapped up the gifts and squirreled them away; she and Daisy went right on wearing what they had. Gifts were pointless. Toto had stuffed every present she'd ever received into the drawers and closets. The house had become a veritable museum of self-denial. In one cubbyhole, Dillon found the chocolate Easter eggs he'd sent the aunts from Dublin a decade before; the chocolate had turned white and "anemic" with age. Six months later, after Toto broke her femur, the aunts would give up the rambling family house and decamp to an apartment. It would then fall to Dillon to clean out the old house so it could be rented. He found Christmas and birthday presents dating from before World War II still sitting on thrones of tissue paper or hidden in their original boxes. He uncovered the sad evidence of his own girlhood, dresses and frilly underwear, a sash with twenty-two Girl Guide badges on it, along with a doll that he remembered Toto had taken away one Christmas and put on a high shelf.

Because Toto was beyond help, Dillon concentrated on nursing Daisy back to health. Every day, Dillon took her out to lunch in town. Toto refused to join them at the restaurant, because she regarded such outings as a shameful waste of money.

Toto, Dillon wrote, "was like a shriveled-up walnut in its shell," withering from starvation, even while she had about twenty-four thousand pounds in the bank (the equivalent of more than a million dollars today). Dillon examined that riddle from the lofty perch of his newfound Gurdjieffian insight: Toto's problem, he decided, was she could not even recognize or name the compulsions that controlled her. She lacked any way to observe, and therefore halt, her own self-destruction. He thought he would escape the fate himself, but he was more like Toto than he realized. "All the Dillons were the same; they lived in poverty and died worth capital in the twenty thousands," he wrote once, about Toto's death, which came a few years later.[4] Little did he realize he was predicting his own end—he would cast aside a fortune of twenty thousand pounds and end his life robed in rags, tortured by starvation, sickened by diseases that only trouble the poor.

* * *

By 1956, Dillon had been letting fate and the shipping lines blow him around the world for years; he'd been attempting to remake himself according to Gurdjieff's teachings, but that had turned out to be difficult indeed. He decided to settle on dry land, to get his bearings and look for a teacher or a group of fellow seekers who could help him with the Work. Dillon quit his ship-doctor job—breaking the contract two years early.

After landing in London, he accepted temporary work at a hospital by the docks while he decided what to do next. The answer came in the form of a book. *The Third Eye* is the autobiography of a "Tibetan" mystic with the improbable name Tuesday Lobsang Rampa; in it, Rampa boasts of his ability to read other people's auras. Immediately upon its publication in 1956, the book created a buzz among amateur mystics; in its first year, it became a massive best seller.

Lobsang Rampa on the cover of the 1966 edition of his best-selling book. Rampa claimed to have endured an operation that opened a hole in his forehead; here, Rampa gets his third eye through the magic of photo-retouching.

Rampa claimed to have born in Lhasa to a noble family who lived in sight of the golden roofs of the Potala. At age seven, he climbed up a mountain road to present himself at the gates of a monastery to train as an adept; during his first year, Rampa distinguished himself among the other Tibetan boys with feats of judo. By his eighth birthday, the lamas had picked him to be one of the rare candidates for an operation to open up his third eye.

Rampa describes that surgery in gruesome detail:

"A strong-looking lama sat behind me and took my head between his knees. The second lama opened a box and removed an instrument made of shining steel. It resembled a bradawl, except that instead of having a round shaft this one was U-shaped, and in place of a point there were little teeth around the edge of the U."[5] A lama pressed this surgical instrument into the boy's forehead. "He applied more pressure, rocking the instrument slightly so that the little teeth would fret through the frontal bone."[6] The boy heard a crunching noise, and the instrument plunged through his forehead, opening up a puncture hole. Into this, the lamas placed a tiny sliver of wood. "Suddenly I felt a stinging, tickling sensation apparently in the bridge of my nose," and then light flashed, and colors whirled in front of him.[7]

"You are now one of us, Lobsang," the chief lama told the boy. "For the rest of your life you will see people as they are and not as they pretend to be."[8] And indeed, the boy now discerned the golden auras vibrating around the bodies of the lamas; and when he left the darkened chamber, he could read the content of character—from hotheadedness to mendacity—in the colors and striations of auras. The boy, with his magical power to look into others' hearts, became an adviser to the Dalai Lama.

In the mid-1950s, Tibet remained a fantastically remote country locked behind icy mountains. Because of its isolation, Westerners were free to imagine it as a Shangri-la of levitating lamas and gold-studded rivers where the usual rules of physics did not apply. Even as late as 1962, Christmas Humphreys, one of Britain's most famous experts on Buddhism, would write, "Nowhere save in Tibet is there so much sorcery and 'black' magic, such degradation of the mind to selfish, evil ends."[9]

Dillon, like nearly all of Rampa's fans, did not suspect a scam when he read *The Third Eye*. He found the book life-changing. Indeed, he must have read *The Third Eye* with a shock of recognition— strip away the Tibetan trappings and the story sounded remarkably similar to his own. Rampa described himself as a survivor of a gruesome surgery performed in secret, a rite of passage that had not just reconfigured his body but also had forever set him apart from others. Rampa advertised himself as a medical miracle, gifted and lonely; Dillon *was* a medical miracle. Recognizing in Rampa a potential soul mate, he sent a fan letter to the author. Oddly enough for a Tibetan lama of his powers, Rampa lived in a flat in Howth, a fishing village in Ireland. Even that did not raise Dillon's suspicions.

And Rampa wrote back! Incredibly, he offered to drop by the London hospital where Dillon was working. One day a potbellied geezer with a shaved head and a gray beard tramped into Dillon's office. Photographs of Rampa show a man who looks like a garden gnome—certainly he did not a cut an imposing figure. Still, his presence electrified Dillon, who after a one-hour interview came away convinced that Rampa could read minds and perhaps even see into the hazy clouds of the future. Rampa had impressed Dillon by flattering him shamelessly, complimenting his intelligence and hinting that he might possess psychic powers. Dillon was hooked.

Weeks later, Rampa wrote to invite Dillon to visit him in the town of Howth, with its sweeping view of Dublin Bay and the little jewel-like island called Ireland's Eye. Dillon jumped at the chance. He'd been laboring for years to find the enlightenment in Gurdjieff's books, with only spotty success. Rampa, on the other hand, promised a shortcut to wisdom.

One day in the summer of 1957, Dillon found himself leaning on the rail of a ship, watching her bow nuzzle the dock at the Dublin Wall. In the days leading up to this trip, he had ached to spend time with Rampa in Howth, but as the moment of reckoning approached, Dillon began to worry. Why had he plunged into this? What, really, had happened that first time he'd met Rampa that had impressed him so? Dillon couldn't remember now. As he stumbled down the gangway to the pier, he wondered whether he'd been a fool to come here. He walked past the dockyard sheds and out onto the road where he found Rampa waiting for him. Dillon was touched by the atmosphere of loneliness that clung to that old man—standing there on the curb, Rampa looked as much a misfit as Dillon himself. All at once, Dillon decided he would trust the old man entirely.

For two weeks, Dillon stayed at a hotel down the road from Rampa's seaside flat; they spent all day together, locked in conversation. They hired a motorboat and puttered along the coast; they drove through the countryside; and all the time, they talked and talked about metaphysics, and morality, and Dillon's Search for Truth. Soon, Dillon was calling the old man Grandpa Rampa. He had found someone to listen to him.

Nights, when they parted, Dillon would let himself into his hotel room and fall into strange dreams. All those two weeks, Dillon sensed the presence of Grandpa Rampa hovering beside him as he slept, guiding him through what Dillon called "astral travels." Unfortunately, he never elaborated on the dreamscapes through which he wandered during those strange slumbers. But whatever he saw convinced him that Rampa possessed powers far beyond the ordinary.

Just before Dillon was to leave Howth, the old man took him out for a drive. At some point, Rampa fixed Dillon with the gaze of his watery blue eyes—and perhaps with his clairvoyant and invisible third eye, too—and announced that he had intuited how Dillon must spend the remaining years of his life. "Do one more sea voyage and then go to India and look for a monastery where you can learn meditation, Michael," Rampa pronounced.[10]

CHAPTER 9
THE CALLING CARD

DILLON SET OUT TO DO JUST THAT. He signed up as the doctor on board a ship that shuttled cargo back and forth between the United States and India; he intended to work for a few years, save up some money, and eventually debark in India and study at a Tibetan monastery.

This is how he ended up on board *The City of Bath* on a May morning in 1958. The sounds of the Baltimore pier filtered in through the porthole of his doctor's office. The air had just turned warm and smelled of all the things he loved: brine and metal and fresh paint.

It appeared that none of the sailors would come in for treatment that morning, and Dillon's mind was just beginning to turn to breakfast when the ship's steward ducked into the office and handed him a telegram from England. Dillon assumed it must be someone sending him word about Grandpa Rampa. In the past months, Rampa had been unmasked, ridiculed, and hung out to dry by the British and German press. They'd tracked down his legal name, Cyril Henry Hoskins, and exposed him as a plumber's son from Devon, England, who'd never set foot in Tibet. Dillon still loved Rampa and continued to believe most of what he'd written. The newspapers often got their facts wrong—Dillon knew that first-hand. He assumed that the press had launched a smear campaign against Rampa, and he was prepared to defend his friend against whatever charges had been raised.

Dillon ripped open the telegram. It was not about Rampa after all. The telegram read, "Do you intend to claim the title since your change-over? Kindly cable *Daily Express*." Dillon's hands began shaking violently. Though he didn't fully understand what this meant, he knew one thing: he'd been found out by the tabloids. What he'd dreaded for fifteen years had finally come to pass. He crumpled up the telegram and threw it into the wastebasket. Just then, one of the crew ducked in to let him know that two reporters were waiting for him on the wharf.

Dillon hid out in his cabin for a while, smoking his pipe and willing his hands to stop trembling. Finally, he decided he had no choice but to submit to the newspapermen. He placed his officer's cap just so on his head—even now, he was careful to adhere to ship rules that stipulated he must never go ashore without his hat. Then he walked down the gangplank, toward the two men, struggling to freeze his face in a blank expression. He thought it best to cooperate. This way, at least, he could have some control over his own image. He found a seat and posed in his starched white uniform, the pipe in one hand, mustering all the dignity he could while the reporters snapped away. He answered their questions with as few words as possible. And when they were done with him, he slunk up the gangway and disappeared into the ship. He thought that was it, that they'd leave him alone now. He believed it was all over.

Dillon wound through the ship's passages until he spotted the captain—the Old Man, as the crew called him. Dillon explained what had happened, revealing himself as a transsexual to his boss. The Old Man simply nodded. There wasn't much that could surprise a ship's captain. Well, the Old Man said, I'd better cable for a police team to guard the gangway because when the evening papers come out, we're going to be mobbed.

In eight hours, his coworkers would learn about the sex change, but for now, no one knew; he remained just an ordinary ship's doctor. He found himself on the upper deck, pacing back and forth, silently repeating a line from one of his Gurdjieff books: "Nothing in life can hurt you if you can learn not to react." The flags on the mast snapped in the spring breeze. Down below, workers scurried around the pier. "Nothing in life can hurt you if you can learn not to react," Dillon repeated to himself, those words the only thing he had to protect himself now. His heart pounded under his starched white uniform shirt. The wind brought tears to his eyes. For years, he'd been training for just this moment, so he could face whatever happened with courage. Nothing in life can hurt you. His heart refused to stop pounding; his hands shook. What had that telegram *meant* anyway? The *Daily Express* editors knew about the sex change, that much was clear; the editors had also mentioned a "title," so they must also have been aware that he was next in line to become baronet of Lismullen. But what else did they know? Who had tipped them off? Had Roberta Cowell sold his story? Would he be stripped of his right to practice medicine? Nothing in life can hurt you, he chanted. Well, it was no use rattling around up here trying to puzzle it out. Gurdjieff and Grandpa Rampa would both agree: he needed to distract himself, to focus his mind. He hurried to the passenger lounge where he found a Scrabble game. He spent the rest of the day playing with a few of the apprentices—forming words, shifting tiles, trying not to think about what was to come.

That evening, Dillon opened up the *Baltimore Sun* to find this short item titled EX-WOMAN (NOW MAN) IN LINE FOR PEERAGE:

> A baronet's sister who changed her sex and reregistered as a male may inherit her brother's title, the editor of *Debrett's Peerage* said today . . . "If a person is registered as a male and recognized by the registrar-general as such, then, as far as I am concerned, that person must be recognized as the heir," commented C. F. Hankinson, editor of *Debrett*.

"It is not too late for me to have a family," said Sir Robert [Dillon] . . . "And of course I can will my estate to anyone I choose. I have no intention of leaving it to my sister—or to my wife. One never does."[1]

And then the next morning, another short piece in the *Baltimore Sun* elaborated:

Dr. Laurence Michael Dillon, calmly puffing on a pipe, told a group of reporters of his life that began 43 years ago as Laura Maude [*sic*] Dillon . . .

Dr. Dillon was surprised at the public disclosure of his sex change. He described the years prior to his operations as "painful ones, emotionally . . ."

He smiled and declined to say if he had considered marriage since his sex change. He said gravely that most of his old friends had deserted him.[2]

The *New York Times* also picked up the item, highlighting it with a headline that blared SEX CHANGE MAKES BRITON HEIR TO TITLE.[3] *Time* magazine, in its brief report on the affair, stressed that Dillon had a good chance of inheriting the family title. "I did not expect my claim would be revealed until my brother's death," Dillon is quoted as saying—one of the few indications that during this period he did indeed expect to become the ninth baronet of Lismullen someday.[4]

After the newspaper stories came out, Dillon holed up in his cabin, afraid to go out on the deck. He wished someone would knock on his door and tell him that the crew had seen the newspapers and they didn't care what anyone said, Dillon was still a good chap. Finally, the third mate ducked into the cabin, bouncing on his toes as he always did. "There's a photographer on the gangway," he said. "What would you like us to do with him?" It was hardly a statement of support, but Dillon took comfort in the way the third mate said it—nonchalantly, as if reporters appeared on the gangway all the time.

Dillon grinned up at the fellow and showed what he wanted by jerking his thumb—throw him off![5]

The third laughed, then disappeared.

Well, there was one ally anyway. The third mate had been born with a harelip. He must have been tormented as a boy, Dillon thought. The third would stick up for him, surely. All the rest of that day, Dillon huddled in his cabin, hoping for another knock on his door, another friend. Silence.

By the next day, he couldn't bear waiting anymore. At noon, Dillon screwed up his courage and knocked on the door of the second mate's cabin—the second had declared twelve o'clock his cocktail hour and had issued a standing invitation to the other officers to come round for drinks.

Come in, come in, the second mate called out, and gestured for Dillon to help himself to a cocktail. The only other man in the room was a crew member named Sparks; both the second and Sparks had smiles pasted on their faces, pretending nothing was wrong, as if they didn't know.

Dillon blurted out a question: Had they seen the newspaper story? They had.

Dillon demanded to know whether they were for him or against him.

In answer, the second mate poured a stiff gin, handed Dillon the glass, then knocked it with his own glass, a silent toast. Thing is, the second said, Sparks and I talked it over last night and we decided you've had a raw deal. We always liked you, and none of this makes a difference to us.

The ship cruised north toward New York, where it docked for ten days of loading. As soon as the gangplank was down, an agent from the Ellerman Lines (the company that owned *The City of Bath*) hurried on board to offer his sympathies to Dillon and to brief him about the situation he'd be facing. The New York police had warned the company that they could not be responsible for protecting Dillon should he leave the ship. Photographers were camping out on the docks, and they planned to get their pictures no matter what. The company had hired a private cop to stand guard on the gangway for Dillon's protection.

That first morning, tired of hiding in his quarters, Dillon climbed to the upper deck to stretch his legs. When he walked to the port side, he caught sight of the crowd below—men, some wearing fedoras, armed with notebooks and cameras and flashbulbs, huddled around the gangway, all waiting for him. Dillon retreated to the starboard side of the deck, out of sight, where he paced back and forth. It was late May now, and hot in the sun. He stripped off his jacket. He felt his panic rising and chanted silently to ward it off: *nothing in life can hurt you.* He still couldn't figure out who'd betrayed him. Who would have leaked his story to the press? He shoved his hands deep into the pockets of his trousers. His black uniform tie jumped in the wind, above his leaping heart. Back and forth he walked, cogitating on his next move.

He could not disembark in New York, that much was obvious. The Yanks had gone mad for transsexuals. Rumor had it they'd strip him naked to see evidence of his sex change. He assumed that if he sailed back to London, he'd be met by a mob of reporters there, too.

Gradually, a plan took shape in his mind. On *The City of Bath*'s first swing past Calcutta, Dillon had disembarked for a few days to look for a monastery run by Tibetans, where he could one day study meditation, just as Rampa had instructed him to do. After asking in a bookshop for a "Tibetan lama," Dillon had found one. Dhardo Rinpoche, an abbot in a yellow silk shirt, chocolate-colored skirt, and Western shoes, had handed him a calling card with the address of a monastery in Kalimpong, India, where monks practiced Tibetan Buddhism.

The calling card, still tucked away among his belongings, offered his escape. He would find this haven in far-off Kalimpong—a place he'd never seen—and throw himself at the mercy of Dhardo Rinpoche. He'd shave off his beard and wear a robe, going incognito, so as to elude the reporters. Grandpa Rampa had predicted that Dillon would take one more sea journey and then study at a monastery in India, and now events were unfolding just as foretold—with a terrible logic that Dillon accepted as his fate. He had expected to travel to India as a Searcher for Truth; but now, as it turned out, he would flee there as a fugitive.

A few days later, Dillon tore open a thick letter from Gilbert Barrow, his old friend from the Bristol garage. Pages covered with Gilbert's handwriting spilled out of the envelope, along with a clipping that explained how the press had discovered Dillon's secret. He hadn't been betrayed by an acquaintance; instead, he'd been betrayed by a clerical error. This he discovered by reading Ephraim Hardcastle's gossip column in the *Sunday Express*. The article described how some astute reporter had discovered a discrepancy between *Debrett's Peerage* and *Burke's Peerage*. *Debrett's* described Sir Robert Dillon as having only one sibling, a brother who would inherit his title; *Burke's* listed Robert Dillon as having a sister. Years before, Michael Dillon had convinced the editor of *Debrett's* to change the entry from "sister" to "brother," and the editor had promised that *Burke's* would follow suit. But *Burke's* hadn't. And that editing oversight had proved to be Dillon's undoing.

Once the discrepancy was discovered, reporters had descended upon Baronet Robert Dillon, demanding an explanation: did he have a sister or a brother, and where was this mysterious person? On the first day, with journalists and photographers swarming him, Bobby revealed only that he had a sister, a doctor in England, and he refused to say where she lived. But by the second day of fending off the reporters, he slipped. He gave the reporters a name: *City of Bath.* Once they knew the ship, all they'd had to do was look up the ship's doctor in the Lloyd's Register and find the name: Michael Dillon. They had him.[6]

Dillon resigned from his job with the Ellerman Lines and from his gentlemen's club in London, assuming that neither institution would want to remain affiliated with him. Instead, both stood by him. The gentlemen's club let him know that nothing had changed—he would remain a member in good standing. And Ellerman Lines urged him to stay on as a ship's doctor. But, wrote Dillon, "it would have been an impossible situation. Boarding any new ship, I would have been the target for speculation and whispers." He'd struggled for fifteen years to blend into the crowd, and he simply could not go back to being a freak, heckled, stared at, and humiliated in the tabloids.[7]

As he saw it, he had only one choice: he had to go into exile before the tabloids found out more of his scandalous story—for instance, the liaison with Roberta. He would disappear to India and dissolve his identity so no one could track him down.

That year, Roberta Cowell declared bankruptcy, carrying a debt to the tune of twelve thousand pounds (the equivalent of about three hundred thousand dollars today). Despite her former achievements as a race-car driver, engineer, and dress designer, she could not find any way to make money. In 1962, Cowell told the London *Times* that as much as she had wanted to work her way out of debt, she was still not able to find any employer willing to associate with her. "Whoever I worked for would have the spotlight on them," she said. "I find it virtually impossible to get a salaried job because there would inevitably be publicity."[8] Cowell—a "spinster," as she was described by the newspaper—had to depend on her parents to support her.

In 1958, Christine Jorgensen was dragging from city to city performing a cabaret act—she belted out G-rated tunes that saucily commented on her past. Jorgensen would much rather have worked as a camerawoman than as a comedienne. But when she tried to get audiences interested in her travel documentary about Denmark— an earnest ode to the lakes and mountains of the country she loved—the crowd laughed her off the stage. No one was willing to hire Jorgensen as anything but a sideshow.

In the 1950s, fly-specked Whites Only signs still dangled over drinking fountains down South; in the cities, homosexual men gathered in underground bars, ears pricked for the clatter of police shoes on the stairs. It was hardly an era known for tolerance. Amidst the vicious bigotry, transsexuals suffered perhaps the most abuse of any minority group of that time. They found themselves barred from almost all jobs; they could not marry without instigating an uproar or a legal battle; and even doctors, the one class of professionals who might have helped them, often treated them as untouchables.

Harry Benjamin was determined to change all that.

By 1952, Benjamin—the endocrinologist who'd administered X-ray "rejuvenating" treatments decades before—had shrunk into a dapper old fellow in a pinstripe suit and silk tie, peering at the world through black-rimmed spectacles. After nearly forty years in the United States, he still retained traces of his German accent, his gallant old-world manners, and a style of dress seldom seen anymore, even in the 1950s: custom-made suits, Sulka ties, and a pocket handkerchief fresh as a just-picked carnation decorating his top pocket.

At the age of sixty-seven, Benjamin had packed up his Park Avenue medical office, preparing to move into smaller rooms on the Upper East Side. "My patients are retiring me," he sighed to his friend Virginia Allen. They'd met for drinks at the Sulgrave Club, in

Dr. Harry Benjamin, the German-born sexologist, created the first standards of medical care for transsexuals. *The Kinsey Institute for Research in Sex, Gender and Reproduction; Harry Benjamin Collection*

a lounge so dark that Allen could hardly see Benjamin's face. As they sat sipping their cocktails in the gloom, he asked if she'd like to come work as his assistant. He only saw a few patients these days, he told her, but he was writing his first book—on prostitution—and he needed someone to type up the manuscript.

Just then the waiter whisked by and left a plate on the table. "What's that?" Benjamin said, squinting down through the cocktail-lounge fog, trying to see the mystery food. He reached into the pocket of his jacket, and a moment later a tiny spot of light danced across the plate. Harry Benjamin was using his throat flashlight to inspect the canapés.

"It would be fun working together, don't you think?" he said to Allen. The spot of light flew upward, toward her face, and darted around her nose and eyes. She was startled and blinked furiously— "dazzled," she wrote later, by both the light and his job offer.

Allen came to work for him in what they called his "retirement office." One day, when she was tidying up, she noticed a collection of files that struck her as odd. Each patient was listed with two names, one male and one female. "What are these few records off by themselves?" she asked.

He glanced at the files. "They're transsexuals and transvestites, some referred by [Alfred] Kinsey. Not very much is known about them," he told her. Benjamin said he had done his best to help these patients, but since he was a specialist in gerontology—using hormones to alleviate the symptoms of old age—he had not been sure how to help the patients that Kinsey had sent him.

"Why don't we do something with [these people], since we have so much time?" Virginia Allen suggested.

"Yes, that may be very good," Benjamin replied. "They are sad people and deserve help, but they make everyone, even other doctors, so nervous and uncomfortable. Bring the records in here and we'll go over them."[9] As little as Benjamin understood these patients, he knew more about them than perhaps any other living physician in the world. During the 1920s, he had made frequent pilgrimages to Vienna so that he could study with Steinach, and during those trips he had called on Magnus Hirschfeld and taken tours of his amazing institute of sexology. He had met transvestites who paraded openly on the streets in petticoats and wigs. In those libertine days in Berlin, cross-dressing was considered a tonic for certain ills of the soul, a medical treatment in its own right. Now Benjamin, one of the few disciples of Hirschfeld's left alive, planned to carry on this grand tradition by helping the patients whom no other doctors would see.

Shortly after Benjamin unretired himself, the Christine Jorgensen story broke. In a matter of months, transsexualism went from obscurity to one of the most-discussed issues in America. When she returned home from Copenhagen in 1953, Jorgensen had discovered bagfuls of mail waiting for her—thousands of people suffering in their own skin, hating themselves for their urges, pleading for her to help them. Among the letters she found one from Benjamin. "Can I be of assistance?" he wrote. "If so please feel free to call on me."[10] She immediately began referring patients to him, turning the dribble of people stopping by his tiny office into a deluge.

Inspired by Benjamin's commitment, Jorgensen decided to use her fame as a megaphone; she aimed to make transsexuality so acceptable that one day it would seem quotidian, just a big yawn. "As you know," she wrote to Benjamin in 1953, "I've been avoiding publicity, but this seems the wrong approach. Now I shall seek it so that 'Christine' will become such an average thing in the public mind that when the next 'Christine' comes along the sensationalism will be decreased."[11] Michael Dillon was one of those next Christines. And indeed, she had softened the blow for him. By 1958, newspaper readers had become slightly less frantic to learn about sex-change operations: his case did not dominate the world headlines or even make page one. Of course, Dillon's story never had a chance to build because he vanished before reporters could get the kind of lurid details they needed to launch a full-scale media whirl. Still, Dillon owed some of his obscurity to Jorgensen: she'd already taken most of the blows.

If Jorgensen hoped to create a world in which transsexuals might live with dignity, Harry Benjamin had even more ambitious plans: he intended to transform the way the medical establishment viewed sex itself. In the early 1950s, he'd begun preaching to his colleagues that no one was entirely male or female. We are all a mix of the two, he argued. Of course, he was hardly the first to make this claim. Hirschfeld had also pushed the idea. So had Freud. But Benjamin had strong visual proof to back up his point. If anyone doubted that one human being can contain elements of both the male and female, Benjamin only had to point to the patients in his waiting room. Here were people taking hormone brews to cross the gender line; in extreme cases, Benjamin recommended his patients fly to Casablanca for castrations and vaginal-construction surgeries that were illegal in the United States. Benjamin could attest that a number of people wished to switch sex, and also that the line between the male and female bodies was fuzzy and easily altered.

"The concept of 'male' and 'female' has become rather uncertain," he wrote in his groundbreaking 1966 masterpiece, *The Transsexual Phenomenon*. He chided the uneducated "man on the street" for believing that every person must be either wholly masculine or feminine. "More sophisticated [people] realize that every Adam contains elements of Eve and every Eve harbors traces of Adam," he wrote.[12] Benjamin had intended his book to be a guide for doctors who were caring for transsexual patients, but in the end, *The Transsexual Phenomenon* is as much a social manifesto as a medical book. "The less we think of the 'opposite sexes,' of the 'war of sexes,' and the more we think of 'human beings' . . . the greater might be the hope of success of a more acceptable civilization than that of today," he exhorted. "Not ashamed of their 'female nature,' men of power might become tamed down, so that the nuclear weapons will not go off."[13]

Benjamin, the social reformer, seemed to be entirely at odds with Benjamin the doctor. On the one hand, he regarded gender roles to be dehumanizing; on the other hand, he helped patients to obtain the surgeries and hormone treatments that would allow them to conform to the very roles he condemned. As a passionate advocate for human rights, Benjamin found himself standing on both sides of the issue. Do sex roles cripple us or do they make us more ourselves? Benjamin didn't seem to know—or perhaps he was compassionate enough to let each patient answer the question for her- or himself. One thing was clear to Benjamin: society needed to recognize that masculinity and femininity come in many shapes and sizes.

Benjamin was not the only one questioning traditional ideas about sex roles. In the 1950s, a group of researchers at Johns Hopkins University—including sexologist John Money—published studies in which they pioneered a new way of speaking about masculinity and femininity. Before the 1950s, *gender* was a word rarely heard outside of language classes, where it was used to discuss rules of grammar in French or Spanish or German. It was Money's idea to apply the word *gender*—and later the terms *gender role* and *gender identity*—to human traits. While a person's biological sex might be male—that is, he might possess XY chromosomes and genitals that produce sperm—it did not necessarily follow that he had a fondness for baseball, bloodred steaks, girlie magazines, or hot rods; he might be a man who preferred a feminine *gender role*. Money's terminology allowed researchers to talk about masculinity and femininity not just as conditions of the body, but also as social constructs and cultural inventions, as roles we play and performances we put on. In the 1960s, Money would help to create the world's first gender-identity clinic, where patients could be trained to conform to the "proper" role. If gender was largely a performance, he reasoned, then anyone could be reprogrammed to conform to the male or female role. Rather than changing society, Money and his colleagues hoped to change people—children especially—to play the parts that had been assigned to them.

By the 1960s, the nascent feminist movement had come to a far different conclusion about gender roles. In her 1963 manifesto, *The Feminine Mystique*, Betty Friedan characterized the female role as a tool of oppression, one that women should cast aside rather than embrace. "In the fifteen years after World War II, this mystique of feminine fulfillment became the cherished and self-perpetuating core of contemporary American culture. Millions of women lived their lives in the image of those pretty pictures of the American suburban housewife, kissing their husbands goodbye in front of the picture window, depositing their station wagons full of children at school, and smiling as they ran the new electric waxer over the spotless kitchen floor," she wrote in the opening paragraphs. "They gloried in their role as women, and wrote proudly on the census blank: 'Occupation: housewife.' " As Friedan saw it, women had colluded in building their own prisons. It was time to break free.[14]

CHAPTER 10
BECOMING JIVAKA

IN THE SUMMER OF 1958, Michael Dillon stumbled up a mountain path. Ahead of him a monk jogged, his yellow robe swirling around his strong calves. Dillon struggled to keep up, gasping in the thin air. Below him stretched the shaggy, terraced slopes of the Tista Valley, and the glittering river that cut through the carpet of trees; in the distance, the white peaks of Kanchenjunga, famed mountain of snows, zigzagged into the sky. But Dillon was in no mood to appreciate the scenery.

For weeks, as he sailed toward India, Dillon had been fixated on the Tibetan teacher Dhardo Rinpoche, and the monastery where he had decided to seek refuge. Over and over, Dillon had comforted himself with a fantasy about Dhardo Rinpoche's warm welcome, and the new life he would start up in the monastery, the hours of meditation and chanting, the mental calm. That very morning, Dillon had finally reached Dhardo Rinpoche's compound. He'd arrived rumpled and exhausted from his journey—a ship to a plane to a bus to a taxi—and he thought surely he'd be hustled in to see Dhardo Rinpoche immediately. Instead, Dillon was left to wait in an antechamber for what seemed like hours. Finally, a monk let him know that the Rinpoche had refused to see him and that he could not stay at the Tibetan monastery after all. Dhardo Rinpoche had instructed Dillon to study among his own kind; he must go live with the English Buddhist who ran a small monastery on top of a

Michael Dillon (now named Jivaka) on the steps of the monastery in Kalimpong. His guru
Sangharakshita sits above him. *From Sangharakshita's private collection, licensed by the Clear Vision Trust*

mountain nearby. The English monk had been ordained in the
Theravada tradition, a sect that stressed conservatism and adhered
to the teachings of the historical Buddha. Dillon dreaded the idea
of studying with an Englishman, especially one who had no access
to Tibetan secrets, those exotic practices that had entranced Dillon
ever since he'd read *The Third Eye*. But he gamely adjusted his expectations and marched up the mountainside, in search of his new
teacher.

The modest red-roofed monastery appeared to be pleasant
enough, with its flowers and its vista of mountains that stretched
all the way to Darjeeling. As Dillon approached, the young Englishman watched him from the porch. From a distance, the monk
could have been an Indian: he wore a yellow robe with one shoulder bare, his head close-shaven, his horn-rimmed glasses obscuring
his eyes. Up close, however, Dillon could see the details that
marked him as a Westerner: the beaky nose and a certain stern expression about the mouth. When the Englishman spoke, it was with
the accent of a working-class Londoner. He introduced himself as

Sangharakshita—years ago, he'd discarded his Western name. He told Dillon he was welcome to live at the monastery as long as he performed chores and contributed a small sum for room and board. The rest of the deal was implied: if Dillon stayed to study and learn meditation, Sangharakshita would become his guru.

Of course, what Dillon needed now was not so much a guru as a protector—someone who could hide him from the reporters and photographers, if they should track him here. Dillon wanted to make sure that Sangharakshita was ready for whatever tabloid chaos he might inflict on the monastery. Without much fanfare, Dillon reached into his wallet and handed the monk a creased newspaper clipping. Sangharakshita read it and then glanced up. He told Dillon it didn't matter—he was free to stay.

Within the next few days, Dillon revealed far more, spilling some of his closest-held secrets. Sangharakshita listened to the confessions with preternatural calm, sharing few of his own thoughts. According to Sangharakshita, "He . . . told me that he had an artificial penis, constructed out of skin taken from different parts of his body. He was very proud of this organ, and offered to show it to me, but I declined the offer . . . He also told me that he was taking hormone tablets to promote the growth of facial hair and to suppress menstruation . . . I asked him why he had wanted to change his sex (not that such a thing is really possible . . .). He said there were two reasons. The first that he felt that he was a male soul imprisoned in a female body. The second was that he had been sexually attracted to women and believed this to be wrong."[1]

In his memoir, Dillon claims that Sangharakshita promised never to repeat his confidences to anyone. "I trusted him because he was both a fellow Englishman and a monk," Dillon wrote.[2]

Sangharakshita, for his part, insists that he never made any such promise about confidentiality. After all, he was not a Catholic priest, obliged to hear confessions under a seal of secrecy; he had no professional obligation to protect Dillon.

Right from the beginning, the two men misunderstood each other completely.

That night, after settling into one of the rooms in the monastery, Dillon pulled out his pipe and stood on the veranda. Instead of lighting up, he hurled it out into the darkness, where it tumbled into the abyss of the valley. In the following days, he would hurl his name away, too—the *Michael* that he'd picked for himself, and the *Dillon* that had linked him to generations of ancestors. He asked Sangharakshita to rename him—not so much for spiritual reasons as practical ones. Dillon was still convinced reporters could track him down, even on this mountaintop.

So Dillon became Jivaka—a name inspired by the doctor who had attended to the Buddha, in a nod to Dillon's medical skills. Weeks or months later, to complete his disappearing act, Dillon shaved his beard. He removed every last piece of evidence that would mark him as that "sex change" in that newspaper clipping, stripping away all the props that he'd adopted years before to help establish his male identity: the pipe, the beard, the Michael. Jivaka would be another sort of person entirely.

Sangharakshita was born Dennis Lingwood in 1925 and grew up roughhousing with the other working-class boys on the streets of Tooting, London. Childhood heart disease—with two years spent in bed—turned him into a reader and introvert. As a teenager, he plowed through *The Diamond Sutra*, an ancient philosophical dialogue, and knew at once that he was a Buddhist. Soon afterward, he received his call-up papers from the British army and was shipped off—conveniently enough—to serve in India. After the war ended, he burned his identity card, deserted from the army, took a new name, and set out to do what mattered. Sangharakshita wandered around the country, often on foot, meditating in caves, begging for food, studying Buddhism. In 1950, he received ordination as a Theravada monk. Seven years later, with the help of donations from friends, he'd managed to buy a retreat with several small bedrooms on a mountaintop in Kalimpong.

In the 1960s, about a decade after he met Dillon, he returned to England and eventually founded his own Buddhist sect, promoting practices and doctrines that he felt would be most suitable for his fellow Westerners. The organization, called Friends of the Western Buddhism Order (FWBO), today boasts thousands of followers. Sangharakshita, now in his early eighties, has retired from his leadership of the FWBO.

He remembers his former student Jivaka vividly. Sangharakshita, after all, has written dozens of books, many of them autobiographical; he has made a study of his own past; in fact, Dillon appears in one of Sangharakshita's autobiographies as an odd, troubled character. When Sangharakshita was asked to provide his recollections of Dillon for this book, he sent lengthy e-mail messages that dripped with a strange mix of pity, fondness, and exasperation—as if, even after five decades, he was still carrying on an argument with his former student.

According to Sangharakshita, Dillon arrived at the monastery still very much under the spell of Grandpa Rampa, still believing in the make-believe Tibet of *The Third Eye*, that fairyland of floating lamas and blue auras. Dillon insisted, too, that Grandpa Rampa had passed on esoteric knowledge to him and that this qualified him to belong to the Secret Order of the Potala, which only had thirteen members—including the Dalai Lama.

Sangharakshita tried to convince Dillon that there was no such secret order. At first, Dillon refused to be talked out of his ideas. He unfurled the proof that the secret order existed—a robe that Rampa had presented to him, and that supposedly conferred membership. Then Dillon gathered the robe around himself, folding it in an origami that Rampa had taught him, and tied it with what appeared to Sangharakshita to be a bathrobe cord.

"But Jivaka, it's an ordinary Burmese monk's robe!" Sangharakshita said.

"No, it's not," Dillon insisted.

Sangharakshita settled the argument by gliding over to a closet and taking out a robe of the same yellow-brown color, identical to the one Dillon wore, right down to the label at the neck.

Eventually, after Sangharakshita argued him out of it, Dillon's trust in Rampa dissolved. With his new teacher's encouragement, he fired off a letter to his former guru, castigating Rampa for telling lies.[3]

That, anyway, is Sangharakshita's version of events. Were Dillon alive today to tell his own story, his account might be very different. In his own writings, Dillon never mentions the Secret Order of the Potala; nor did he appear to hold any grudge against his old teacher, even at the end of his life. "Much of what [Rampa] told me purporting to be of his own life I now know to be false," Dillon acknowledged, but still "what he said of the universe and man's place in it made good sense."[4] And Dillon insisted that his time with Rampa had not been wasted—he still loved the old man.

So it's unclear whether Dillon did come to India convinced that Rampa had inducted him into a secret order of adepts with a special handshake and costume. Of course, whether Dillon fully believed in it or not, the Secret Order of the Potala was an apt metaphor for his situation. Dillon *did* belong to a secret organization with only about a dozen members worldwide. He *did* have special knowledge. Unlike nearly everyone else alive during his time, he knew what it was like to live in both a male and a female body. No one around Dillon seemed to grasp that his experience had given him unique insight into the human condition. Dillon himself, then, would have to find other ways to prove he had special powers.

He had grown up an orphan, but now, in India, he had become an orphan in the most profound sense. He had lost not only his family and friends, but also his country and his name. He was a man in exile, and he craved, more than ever, to belong to someone or something. At first, he did belong to Sangharakshita, who included him in morning rituals, showed him how to meditate, and assigned him chores.

Sangharakshita was finishing up a book, a memoir that would explain how he'd come from Tooting to live on a mountaintop in India. Dillon became his secretary. Even though he'd been educated at Oxford, versed in Greek and Latin, and had already published his own book, Dillon performed the menial work without complaint. He was eager to please his new teacher: "There was . . . a definite streak of sentimentality in his character and a strong craving for affection."[5]

During those long, slow afternoons at Kalimpong, in between typing drafts for his guru, Dillon began to work on his *own* autobiography. In his own manuscript, titled "Out of the Ordinary," he struggled to make sense of all that had happened to him, pouring out the very secrets that he'd come to India to protect. "Michael Dillon" had been snuffed out and replaced by Jivaka—except in the manuscript. Day after day, the pile of delicate onion-skin pages grew taller; inside those pages, Dillon was able to reinvent and reimagine the life he'd just escaped, to make himself the hero of that English existence.

Dillon does not say why he began writing, whether he wanted to set the record straight or simply document an extraordinary life. At any rate, he typed and typed. He lavished special care on his childhood, dedicating many pages to the amber glass of a certain door in the aunts' house and the Victorian gloom of the nursery and the querulous voices of the grown-ups. Just when he'd lost Bobby and Aunt Toto and all of England for good, he found himself washed over with memories of his childhood.

When Dillon stepped away from the desk, he remained a child of sorts. His guru expected him to obey orders, eat whatever he was served, and sleep where he was given a bedroll. He had become Sangharakshita's boy.

Later in his career in India, Dillon would describe the relationship between a disciple and his lama (or guru) in the Tibetan tradition: "The reverence is absolute. The student or disciple makes the triple obeisance each day on his first meeting his Lama; he must never share his master's seat nor sit at a higher level ... The Lama ... owns [the disciple] utterly ... The Lama may treat [the disciple] as he thinks fit, because he will know what is best for his spiritual development."[6]

Sangharakshita, who practiced in the Theravada tradition, did not demand that kind of extreme deference. Still, he was happy to play the role of master, more Dillon's boss than his teacher. Dillon was isolated on a mountaintop, lost in a land where he could not speak the language, and dependent on Sangharakshita for food and shelter. He began to look up to Sangharakshita in the same way he had once revered Rampa.

Soon the two men had forged an intimate and strange relationship. Dillon began to call his guru "Daddy"—an endearment that Sangharakshita apparently tolerated. "I did not really like [it], especially as he was ten years older than me," according to Sangharakshita. But he didn't tell Dillon to stop.[7]

Winter came. Sangharakshita would be traveling around India, giving lectures, until the spring. He would not take Dillon along. Instead, he had decided to deposit Dillon in the care of some Theravada monks in Sarnath, as one might leave a boy with trusted friends. Dillon appears to have had little say in the matter.

Sarnath, where the Buddha delivered his first sermon, sits close to the holy city of Varanasi; it is a popular destination for religious pilgrims, with its collection of half-ruined stupas, towers, sculptures, bas-relief portraits of the Buddha, and warrens of ancient monasteries. Dillon landed here at the end of 1958, staying at the hostel run by the Maha Bodhi Society. Several Theravada monks would act as his advisers and allow him to observe their morning rituals in the local temple.

In his letters to Sangharakshita—or "Daddy"—Dillon invented a whole system of nicknames for the august monks of Sarnath. The most senior monk at the local temple, the Venerable Sasanasiri, became H.P., for "high priest"—a nickname that made him sound more American industrialist than religious leader. Sangharakshita notes that Dillon loved such pet names; they were a sign of belonging, and clubbiness, a relic of the elite British boys' schools he was never able to attend as a child.

At first in Sarnath, Dillon ached with loneliness. "You can't make friends when you have nothing in common and no mutual language," he wrote to Sangharakshita.[8] His schedule, however, left him with little time to feel abandoned. He arose early for rituals in the temple, then meditated, and studied and wrote for the rest of the day—working as furiously as he ever had in medical school, perhaps even more so.

In Kalimpong, Sangharakshita had allowed his student to read only one or two elementary books on Buddhism. He insisted that Dillon was not ready to tackle the more abstruse teachings. But at the Maha Bodhi Society, Dillon found a library of astonishing breadth—it included English translations of many of the Buddhist classics. Dillon crammed, learning about the different sects of Buddhism, the essential tenets of the religion, the history of India. This was something he knew how to do—take in knowledge from the page. With books strewn all around his little monastic cell and notes piling up beside a borrowed typewriter, he began to grow ambitious. Why remain Sangharakshita's typist? Couldn't he aspire to one day enjoy the kind of life Sangharakshita led—as a teacher and author, a Western expert on Buddhism, even a monk?

The tone of his letters to Sangharakshita changed; he sometimes dared to tease and sass his guru. In January of 1959, he asked "Daddy" whether, in his travels, he had found himself "so much in demand as a lecturer still? Or have you succumbed to soft and riotous living?"[9]

At times, in his long letters, Dillon quarreled with Sangharakshita in the way that one does with an absent friend, taking both sides of the argument himself. Dillon adored Christmas, even though—or perhaps because—he'd spent so many holidays alone. He fetishized those trappings of family Christmases that he'd so often been denied: plum puddings and presents and a big hearty supper surrounded by kin. Sangharakshita had apparently informed Dillon that, as a Buddhist, he would have to give up Christmas, which bothered Dillon immensely. "Master, do you think some of your ideas need a bit of adjusting??? I think there must be a happy medium between your attachment to anti-Westernism and mine to pro-Westernism."[10]

Still, Dillon was not always so high-handed—indeed he aspired to the kind of humility that the Buddhist texts celebrated. He had begun to realize just how much work he'd have to do to overhaul his mind, to strip it of the snobbishness that had been drummed into him by the aunts and English society. He acknowledged that he found it difficult to make his ceremonial bows before the Sarnath monks who were his superiors. It is hard, he noted, for an Englishman to get on his knees—particularly when he was bending before a dark-skinned man. A rhyme about "dusky Indians" that he'd learned as a child kept going round and round in his head maddeningly, and he could not seem to silence it. Dillon had become aware that his white skin created a barrier to spiritual attainment, and he did his best to cast his privilege away.

"It is not easy to change at my age but that does not mean it is impossible," he wrote to Sangharakshita. "Obviously I've changed a lot in the last six years,* but it is harder [for me] than it was for you . . . since you didn't have the traditions of the British aristocracy rammed into you from the early years. Indeed, for you, reaction meant the opening up of class-consciousness . . . I look forward to the day I can go with you as your junior assistant on one of those tours [to minister to impoverished Indians]—when all of these British prejudices are removed!"[11]

He had always hungered for badges of belonging: gold braid, uniform jackets, rowing caps, insignia. On the mantel of his house in Ireland, he had placed photos of his rowing team, himself in a line of brothers. Now, once again, he wished desperately to be an insider. But instead of a team or a club, he had set his sights on the Buddhist monastic community, and on the yellow robe that would mark him as a Theravada monk. As much as he'd once longed to wear a sailor's uniform, Dillon now ached for the robe that would allow him to match the other men who sat in rows in the temple. He would melt in among them, and finally, he'd belong.

The first step toward full-fledged monkhood would be to take vows as a novice monk. It was a simple matter to become a novice— any teenaged boy could earn the title by participating in a short ceremony. The supplicant would be presented with a robe and shown how to fold it, then asked to repeat a series of vows, one of which was to abstain from holding property. For most novices—boys who

---

*Dillon seems to have considered 1952, when he'd first discovered Gurdjieff's books, as the date of his first step onto the spiritual path. By his count, then, he'd been struggling to retrain his mind for the last six years.

owned nothing besides a few rupees—that promise would be easy enough to keep. For a man in his forties with no steady income nor any family nearby, a man who could not speak the local language nor understand the customs, the vow was tantamount to cutting off a lifeline. Dillon could have bent the rules by asking a friend back in England to hold his money for him, but he did not. He could have reserved an emergency fund, a cushion. Instead, Dillon plunged into his new faith with self-destructive abandon, tossing away all his belongings. He wrote to his lawyers back in England and asked them to give his savings and his inheritances to charity; his trustees were so stunned by their client's request that they dawdled for nearly a year before obeying his wishes. It was an astoundingly reckless move, especially because Dillon had amassed a fortune amounting to twenty thousand pounds by now. The bulk of it he'd inherited from Toto, who had died just a few years before.

Dillon does not say much about what would become one of the most drastic decisions of his life—a decision as irreversible, in its way, as the sex change. He seems to have had no idea just how difficult it would be to survive on his wits in India. He was modeling himself on Sangharakshita, who despite his vow of poverty had nonetheless wound up with a rather enviable writing career as well as proprietorship of a monastic compound. Dillon imagined that he could follow a similar path—he was already churning out articles about Buddhism for papers in India and sending off columns to spiritual newsletters back in England. And he'd banged out a book, too, a sort of Buddhism-for-beginners title, *Practicing*. He sent out the book under his new name, Jivaka. It was printed only in India—and badly at that. Nonetheless, he'd pulled off a rather remarkable feat for someone so new to life as a Buddhist—after only a few months of study, he'd fobbed himself off as an expert. There was more than a dash of arrogance to Dillon's new pose—clearly, he remained as much a know-it-all as he'd had been when he'd paced around the garage, lecturing Gilbert Barrow about philosophy. At the same time, Dillon had no other way to make money besides becoming an author. "The only possible source of income for me was writing."[12] He could not work as a doctor anymore; to do so, he would have to use the name Michael Dillon and risk discovery; furthermore, he'd learned that the Buddha forbade monks from charging money for medical services.

Spring came, and Dillon left Sarnath to return to Kalimpong and take up his life again there as Sangharakshita's protégé. He donated his last possessions—the 150 pounds he had left over from ship's wages as well as a gold signet ring—to Sangharakshita's monastery. (Sangharakshita, for his part, denies that Dillon made any such gifts.) Dillon had been looking forward to settling into his old room at the monastery, particularly now that he wore the robe of a novice monk. If he hewed to his vows for a year or so, he might be allowed to take the "higher ordination" and become a full-fledged monk. He expected Sangharakshita would recognize him as someone who could one day become an equal.

The guru did not. As Sangharakshita saw it, Dillon was a woman, and therefore completely unfit to take vows in the male community. To this day, Sangharakshita believes that a sex change does nothing to alter an individual's identity. "Jivaka was not able to beget a child [as a man]. To my mind it is this factor that determines the gender to which one belongs."[13]

They had an argument: Sangharakshita remembers it had to do with one of the local boys who had come to live at the monastery; Dillon threw a shoe at the guru's new protégé. Whatever the reason for the rift, it was inevitable. Dillon chafed under the guru's rules. After a few months, he announced he would leave Kalimpong and return to the hostel in Sarnath, where he had recently enjoyed so much independence. And so, in the fall of 1959, he packed up his meager belongings and left his manuscript, the one that told his secrets, in a trunk that belonged to Sangharakshita.

Dillon returned again to Sarnath, to study and meditate—and to contemplate how he might bend the rules governing who could and could not become a monk. Dillon did not worry about the restriction against women; he assumed that most other Buddhists would regard him as a man, albeit as an unusual kind of man. But he had discovered another law in the monastic code that alarmed him. It forbade anyone who belonged to the "third sex" from the higher ordination. It's not clear what the twenty-five-hundred-year-old religious codes meant by the term *third sex*—the phrase may have been a catchall for intersexuals, cross-dressers, and gay men. But whatever the third sex might be, the ancient writings made clear that these people could not become monks. Of course, Buddhist law also banned dwarves, epileptics, and even sufferers of boils, eczema, and goiter from the monastic community. Dillon assumed that modern Buddhist leaders must have decided to overlook some of these rules. He asked one of the Theravada monks whether men with war injuries would be barred from ordination and got just the answer he wanted: not anymore.[14] That gave Dillon the courage to approach H.P. and other local holy men and confess that he belonged to the third sex (without giving them the details of his situation). Would they give him the higher ordination? The superiors weighed in: the English novice would never become a Theravada monk.

Dillon was devastated. For the rest of his life, he would denounce the Theravada tradition as rigid and hierarchical. It was then that he resolved to switch his affiliation and throw his lot in with the Tibetans. Perhaps the red-robed Tibetan monks would recognize him as a man.

Of course, it was his fascination with Tibetan Buddhism that had drawn him to India in the first place, and during his stay in Sarnath, he had plunged into study of their tradition. Dillon had been lucky to strike up a friendship with Professor Herbert V. Guenther, then in residence at nearby Sanskrit University. A German-born professor two years Dillon's junior, Guenther would become one of the preeminent translators of Tibetan Buddhist texts. At that time, he was still a young teacher, happy to chat with anyone who dropped by.

On a sweltering day in November 1959, Dillon arrived at Guenther's office for lunch. That afternoon, the professor spun a tale about a fabled monastery called Rizong. It was located in Ladakh, a country on the Tibetan border. High up in the Himalayas, in an aerie that was nearly impossible to reach, the monks of Rizong practiced Tibetan Buddhism in its most pure and punishing form, adhering rigidly to rules set down centuries before. At Rizong monastery, "if a monk goes out and returns with his robes not absolutely correctly arranged, he gets a nice beating at the gate," Guenther said. "And if [the monks] have been drinking alcohol they get a hundred lashes."[15]

Guenther had never been to this monastery, which would at that time have seemed an impossible destination; India controlled Ladakh and kept the borders tightly sealed from its rival, China. Certainly, no Englishman would be welcome there. Rather, Guenther offered up Rizong as a fable, a vision of monastic Buddhism taken to its furthest extreme. Dillon accepted the story in that spirit—Rizong, like Tibet itself, seemed as much an idea as it was an actual place.

Over and over during the next year, Dillon would continue to hear rumors about Rizong monastery. The locals told him it was famous for two things: its severe punishments and its fruit trees. Dillon had begun to long for exactly that—a place of strict fathers and sweet rewards.

In March 1959, the Dalai Lama made his famous escape from Chinese-occupied Tibet, climbing vertiginous Himalayan paths to avoid detection by border guards. A week later, Premier Zhou Enlai declared the Chinese-installed government of Tibet to be the true one; Tibet, as a self-ruled country, ceased to exist. Fleeing their homes, Tibet's most talented leaders and intellectuals scattered across India. It was an enormously exciting and poignant time to be a Western student of Tibetan Buddhism in India.

In the fall of 1959—the year Tibet dissolved as a country and began to exist as a dream—Dillon lived in Sarnath, surrounded by glamorous refugees. It was the Tibetans of the Geluk sect, or "yellow hats," who most struck a chord with him. They had been Tibet's philosophers and bookworms—its "Oxford men." And now they had flooded into town to eke out an existence, arriving dizzy with grief and hunger.

One of Dillon's neighbors, Locho Rinpoche, had once taught at Lhasa's top university, where he was considered the reincarnation of a famous scholar. Now he subsisted in abject poverty. "It seemed that my world was falling apart," Locho would write many years later. "I kept thinking of all the things that we had done wrong when we still had a country and went over all the ways we could have avoided the final catastrophe, until I nearly drove myself mad with regret and frustration."[16]

Dillon venerated Locho and the other Tibetans, without guessing the self-doubt and vertiginous loss these men felt as refugees. "Never could more men of high spiritual development have been found gathered in one place," he wrote.[17] The presence of these holy men gave Dillon a new sense of purpose. He suddenly discovered himself to be enormously busy, helping with the preparations for the Dalai Lama's upcoming visit. He provided free medical services to anyone who needed them and labored with the other pilgrims to fashion thousands of butter lamps for endless rituals and prayer sessions the Dalai Lama would attend.

After months of malnutrition, he had become a beaky, bald-headed, emaciated fellow in a frayed yellow robe, his face clean-shaven to reveal the hollows of his cheeks. He lived at the Maha Bodhi Society hostel subsisting on a few rupees—so little that he had trouble paying the postage due when his old tutor Jimmy McKie sent him packages of food from England. "Jivaka seems to have been a misguided idealist and gave whatever assets he had to the [Maha Bodhi] Society," according to Professor Guenther. "Jivaka . . . was a constant guest at our house and we looked after his dietary needs."[18]

Dillon had grown so thin and sun-scorched that he blended into the crowd of monks swirling through Sarnath. Only those surprising blue eyes set him apart. European and American tourists noticed those eyes and wanted to learn his story. How had he come to be here, in a monk's robe? Would he pose for a photograph? Dillon shrugged them away. One thing was sure: no one would ever recognize him as Michael Dillon. He had reinvented himself as Jivaka, the spiritual seeker with pale skin and an unfathomable past. And now he wanted to go further than any Westerner had ever been.

Dillon aspired to become the first Englishman to belong to the Tibetan monastic community. It was a tall order—to belong to a people whose language he couldn't speak and whose government had dissolved. Even though the cult of Tibet had swelled in Europe and the United States, no Westerner had ever managed to become a monk in that tradition. The high peaks of the Himalayas, the troops patrolling the borders, the language difficulties—such barriers had kept foreigners at bay.

Dillon, however, had reason to hope he might succeed where others had failed. He had befriended a man named Lama Lobzang, who volunteered to become his translator and, indeed, to take on the Englishman as his special project. A pint-size monk in a scruffy, informal summer robe, Lama Lobzang might not look like a power broker, but in fact he knew everyone in Sarnath, spoke a smattering of languages, and could make the wheels turn for people he liked. He held special sway among the Tibetan dignitaries, to whom he brought endless *tsompa* and tea to keep them from starving. Perhaps most propitiously, Lama Lobzang hailed from Ladakh, the tiny border country near Tibet where one still might find a traditional monastery such as Rizong. As Lama Lobzang saw it, Dillon needed to be ordained as a Tibetan Buddhist for practical as well as spiritual reasons. The Indian military would forbid an Englishman—a potential spy—from traveling through the Himalayas, and therefore, from living in most Tibetan monasteries. However, if Dillon identified himself as a monk, he might be able to obtain a permit.

Lama Lobzang set to work seeing what he could do to wrangle an ordination for Dillon; since the Englishman had already apprenticed himself for months as a Theravada novice monk, he was considered a good candidate for full ordination in the Tibetan tradition. Lama Lobzang talked to Locho Rinpoche about performing the ceremony; he must have been persuasive because soon Locho offered to set a date for Dillon's induction into the Tibetan tradition.

Before that happened, Dillon felt duty-bound to inform both Lama Lobzang and Locho Rinpoche that he belonged to the third sex. He did his best to explain the situation in rudimentary Hindi and English. Neither man seemed to regard his status as an impediment to his becoming a monk. But, then again, Dillon wasn't sure they'd understood him. Lama Lobzang spoke only broken English; Locho spoke none at all.

To make sure everything was on the up-and-up, Dillon wrote a letter to Sangharakshita, asking him to come to Sarnath to act as an English-to-Hindi translator and to preside at the ceremony. Somehow, in the months since he'd left Kalimpong, Dillon had convinced himself that Sangharakshita—his "Daddy"—would be proud of him.

CHAPTER 11
A NEW AGE

THE REPLY WAS HARDLY WHAT DILLON HAD EXPECTED. Sang-harakshita fired back a letter, in triplicate, to Lama Lobzang, Locho Rinpoche, and H.P., the top local monk in Sarnath. His letter revealed Jivaka's Western name and spilled details of the sex-change operation. And, according to Dillon, it included many false accusations as well. Sangharakshita spread his message so effectively that even Professor Guenther, living in the nearby city of Varanasi, heard the gossip. "I knew that [Dillon] was a woman-turned-man," according to Guenther. He also heard "that [Dillon's] sex organ was diminutive."[1]

Nowadays, Sangharakshita still believes that he had no choice but to write the letter. Dillon intended to break monastic law, and Sangharakshita refused to be a party to that. Dillon could not understand that moral logic and "therefore felt not only angry but also betrayed," according to Sangharakshita.[2]

Betrayed indeed. One Saturday morning, Locho Rinpoche handed Dillon the letter from Sangharakshita and explained (as Lama Lobzang translated) that the ordination was off. Locho had no objections to Dillon becoming a monk. But it would be too politically dangerous to go ahead with the ordination when someone as prominent as Sangharakshita opposed it. As Dillon reeled at the news, Locho tried to comfort him, assuring the Englishman that he would get his ordination one day. Eventually the hullabaloo over

Dillon's third-sex status would have to die down, and then he could quietly become a monk, Locho promised.

Still, Dillon was distraught. As he saw it, Sangharakshita had meant to do more than prevent his ordination; he'd meant to tarnish Dillon's reputation in the Buddhist community. If his former teacher had merely wanted to put a stop to the ceremony, he could have written a letter stating that Dillon was not a suitable candidate—and only hinted at the reasons why. Instead, Sangharakshita had dropped a bomb. Handwritten addenda in Dillon's manuscript indicate that he believed Sangharakshita had also sent a letter to Christmas Humphreys, one of the most prominent of the British Buddhists, and also to a Buddhist journal called the *Middle Way*. Dillon feared the letters would put an end to his writing career—and his meager livelihood.

In fact, he had just entered into negotiations with the venerable British press John Murray to publish a book on the life of Milarepa, a Tibetan saint. He planned to publish the book as "Jivaka"—under that name, he had no history. Luckily, his secret had not yet spread beyond a small circle of men in the Buddhist community. Dillon hoped to keep it that way. He thought he could remain incognito if he burrowed in among the Tibetan Buddhists; his new friends seemed willing to overlook his third-sex status and be eager to help him on his path. A Tibetan monastery seemed the last place left where he could hide out and remain the person he felt himself to be.

While Dillon was madly looking for a way to become a monk, a new year had dawned. It was 1960 now. In the coming decade, British and American attitudes about transsexuality would undergo a radical shift. The sex-change operation would become legal in both countries; more than that, it would also acquire a certain cachet as a high-profile surgery, performed at some of the world's top hospitals.

Dillon had learned to see himself as branded with a secret so outrageous, so unique, that it would make worldwide news if it was revealed. But Dillon's secret was already beginning to lose some of its power. As the years went on, it became less and less likely that, had he been exposed, a crowd of journalists would have chased him to India. His unfathomable transformation was turning into just another medical procedure. Indeed, many nontranssexuals were using hormone pills and surgeries to sculpt their bodies. And transsexuals were becoming more numerous every day.

By the early 1960s, men who wanted to become women had beaten a path to Tijuana or Casablanca, where genital surgeries were legal; or they'd resorted to underground surgeries. This system infuriated a small cadre of American doctors and psychiatrists. These professionals felt that *they* should be the ones ministering to transsexuals and performing the miraculous surgeries, and they should be able to do it legally; therefore, they pushed for new standards that would bring the sex-change operation to their own hospitals.

John Money, the researcher who'd coined the term *gender role,* became the mastermind behind new policies at Johns Hopkins that led to the first aboveboard sex changes in the Unites States.* In the early 1960s, at Money's insistence, the hospital formed a committee to

---

*While John Money became an advocate for surgeries that benefited transsexuals, in the larger scheme of things he should not be considered a promoter of tolerance for transgendered and intersexed people. Money pioneered "gender therapies" that forced children—those deemed sissies and tomboys—to conform to traditional roles. Sometimes these therapies involved humiliation, verbal abuse, and even physical abuse. Also, Money relentlessly pushed a rigid two-gender system in which every person, even infants, had to adhere to either male or female body types. He became one of the loudest voices calling for cosmetic surgeries on infants with ambiguous genitalia, surgeries intended to make nontraditional genitals appear to be "normal." The Intersex Society of North America considers such cosmetic surgeries on children and infants to be a human rights violation; the group argues for patient-centered care of intersexed people, rather than care that reflects the desires of doctors and parents. See John Colapinto's book *As Nature Made Him: The Boy Who Was Raised as a Girl* for more about John Money's role in the medical treatment of people with ambiguous genitals.

examine the legal and moral issues surrounding sex-reassignment surgery. This committee interviewed several well-groomed, attractive "girls" that Harry Benjamin had brought to Baltimore. They were all male-to-female transsexuals who'd gone abroad for their operations and who had flourished in their new lives as women. And they must have been convincing. After a yearlong investigation, the hospital committee determined that the operations would not violate Maryland law or medical ethics.

As soon as the Johns Hopkins committee decided to okay the surgeries, it then had to define just what exactly a "sex change" might be. Was the switch purely physical, or did it require a mental shift that should be overseen by psychiatrists? What, besides the obvious, was the goal of a sex change? What constituted a "successful" performance of the male or female role?

The committee decided that only those patients who were able to shine in their new role would be allowed into the operating room. To qualify for treatment, a patient would have to prove his dedication by living as his or her intended sex for an entire year—a nearly impossible feat for some people. Johns Hopkins rejected one client because he worked as a (male) bank teller during the day and a cosmetics saleslady at night; though, really, how else was he to afford the staggering cost of the treatments?

With hundreds of people begging for surgery, and with so few spots available, the hospital could afford to be choosy about its patients. Anyone whom the Johns Hopkins psychiatrists deemed an eccentric, a troublemaker, or a loudmouth would be sent away. Only a dozen or so patients could be operated on every year.

To screen the patients, the committee set up the Gender Identity Center, the first of its kind in the world, which included a team of psychiatrists to establish what "normal" gender roles might be and then make sure patients conformed to them. Johns Hopkins researchers would continue to monitor the patients for years after their operations to determine whether they had indeed "succeeded" as men and women. This research into the psychological aspects of transsexualism was largely bankrolled by a shadowy benefactor named Reed Erickson. The *New York Times* referred to him as a "consulting engineer of independent wealth"[3]; the newspaper did not mention that Erickson was a transsexual man, the first person ever to legally switch from female to male in the United States. Johns Hopkins surgeons had overseen his transformation.

"The Johns Hopkins Hospital has quietly begun performing sex change surgery," reported the *New York Times* in 1966.[4] Indeed, the announcement of the first legal sex change in America was a pin drop compared to the hullabaloo that had surrounded Christine Jorgensen's operation in the 1950s. And so, with hardly a murmur, the sex change became just another medical procedure. By the time newspapers announced the new Gender Identity Center at Johns Hopkins, ten sex changes had already taken place, and three of the patients had married. Other hospitals hurried to follow Johns Hopkins's example. Within a few years, Stanford University, the University of Minnesota Medical School, and Northwestern University Medical School had set up gender clinics and were performing sex changes. In 1967, British surgeons at Charing Cross Hospital also began performing the operations.

There had been no legal battle. The tabloid papers hardly bothered to notice. Religious leaders looked the other way. Representatives of Baltimore Protestant and Jewish clergy announced that they had no moral objections; the Catholics declined to comment. What had caused a scandal a decade before now seemed to provoke little more than a raised eyebrow.

But then, of course, cosmetic surgery and hormone treatments no longer seemed so terribly outré; millions of people were using these "technologies of appearance," as they might be called, to resculpt themselves. Housewives who wanted Jayne Mansfield breasts or Marilyn Monroe lips sidled into clinics and asked if there was any hope; grandmothers who wanted to hold on to their youth began popping a daily hormone pill, a pill that doctors promised contained the key to both soft skin and a sparkling personality. Transsexuals weren't the only ones who felt trapped in their body and humiliated by the way they looked; millions of nontranssexuals, particularly women, also felt this way. During the 1960s, some patients began to depend on medicine to do more than just heal; now it could also fix a broken identity.

Despite the popularity of hormone therapies and cosmetic surgeries, the "sex-change operation" had lodged in the public mind as a magical transformation, something entirely different from the medicine used by nontranssexuals. Though millions of people had now resorted to the same kind of treatments that Christine Jorgensen had used to manipulate her body, Americans were still tittering with nervous laughter over Christine's medical high jinks. In the early sixties, dozens of Christine jokes circulated in locker rooms. One such gag has Christine in bed with a new husband; when she examines his goods, she is clearly disappointed. She quips, "I *threw away* more than that."[5]

The joke speaks to the terror some men must have felt at the idea of Christine look-alikes circulating in bars and strip clubs. These transsexuals might be able to pass as born women, as—hell!— gorgeous women who would seduce you. Transsexuals inspired flights of paranoia in the early sixties, largely because of their ability to "trick" straight men.

"Ah, friend, they are the great masqueraders of the world. They live in that umber land where illusion and reality, identity and anonymity, death and rebirth, mingle and diffuse," wrote Tom Buckley in a 1967 *Esquire* article.[6] Buckley laid out the figures that might have terrified his readers: There were about four hundred male-to-female transsexuals living in the United States, and nobody knew who they were. You could not tell them apart from natural-born women, because their "femininity will withstand all but the closest gynecological scrutiny."[7] You, he implies, might end up sleeping with one of them. There it was. Out in the open. The great fear. Four hundred ex-men like booby traps set around the country. He portrays transsexuals as imps, tricksters, spies in the house of love. And he admits that he doesn't like the specimens that he's met. "In my conversations with transsexuals who had already undergone surgery, I sensed a colossal self-righteousness . . . On my part, I suppose, there was an underlying prejudice against what could be called deserters from the male sex."[8]

Of course, with such powerful hatred directed at them, transsexuals had no choice but to hide in the crowd. It was nearly impossible in the 1960s to find work if you were known to be a transsexual. In 1966, Harry Benjamin reported that out of fifty-one of the male-to-female patients he'd studied, nine had resorted to prostitution to keep themselves fed.

A "successful" male-to-female transsexual, according to most doctors of the 1960s, was someone who could erase her past, settle primly behind a picket fence, wear tasteful Chanel suits and coral-pink lipstick, marry a breadwinner, and conduct herself with white-glove manners; doctors seemed to feel betrayed when their patients failed to live up to this rather narrow standard of success. Benjamin defended the rights of M-to-F transsexuals to become prostitutes, but he was clearly disturbed that many patients had taken up dangerous and illegal work.

He was far happier with the outcomes of his F-to-M patients. "Bobby is now reasonably successful as an architect," he writes of one of the cases he followed. Another is "a man in his early forties, of some importance in the art world, married to a highly intelligent woman and living in an environment where very few of the numerous friends of this couple have any idea of the husband's past." Yet another had become a successful businessman, with many friends who "don't know."[9]

The F-to-Ms often enjoyed greater status and earning power after their transition than they had before; the mid-1960s was still the era of businessmen and secretaries, of men in skyscrapers and ladies in the home. To transform into a man was to suddenly be pegged at a higher value. Benjamin wondered why more women didn't do it; he mulled over a Gallup poll that had found that surveyed women would rather have been born men by a margin of twelve to one; most of those women were tired of being treated like second-class citizens, but surely at least a few of them had a deeper itch for a male identity. And yet, in the 1960s, few women came into Benjamin's office begging to be made into men. Benjamin had a theory for this: The tabloids had yet to seize on a male equivalent of Christine Jorgensen. No trans man had become a superstar, showing off what testosterone and surgery could do, and making the metamorphosis seem possible.[10]

In fact, those few transsexual men who did exist in the sixties seemed to have a talent for disappearing into the mainstream, for joining the three-piece-suit march of executives down the sidewalk. Of course, they had even more to lose than did M-to-Fs if they were exposed—not just their status as "normals" but also their male privilege.

As Benjamin and his colleagues saw it, a successful transsexual man should be a skilled impostor. He shouldn't tell big lies, mind you, just a string of little ones: Girl Scout camp become Boy Scout camp, and a women's college became a men's university, and a year in the hospital became a stint in the army. The doctors saw those cover-ups as proof of a transsexual man's psychic strength, his commitment to his new role. They didn't understand just how agonizing it might be for these men to misrepresent themselves to friends, the terror of building a career that could be destroyed in an instant.

By the standards of the 1960s medical community, Michael Dillon would have been deemed a resounding success because, despite all the close calls, he'd managed to masquerade as a born man. For fifteen years, he had passed; and when the tabloids had exposed him, he'd fled to India and taken up a new name and identity. And now that his secret had leaked out in Sarnath, and he was in danger of being recognized as a transsexual in India, he was trying to run again, to a Tibetan monastery, preferably in the remote country of Ladakh. He hoped to set himself up in one of the most remote out-backs in the world, on a road so perilous that it was blocked by snowdrifts during most of the winter. In such a Tibetan monastery, beyond the reach of newspapers and gossip, he hoped to find the one last place in the world where he could exist as himself.

CHAPTER 12
RIZONG

IN EARLY 1960, Dillon managed to wrangle a meeting with Kushok Bakula, a prince in the royal family of Ladakh. The prince could grant Dillon what he most wanted: an ordination as a Tibetan monk and a passport into Ladakh. Dillon poured out his story to the prince and was enormously comforted by the way Kushok Bakula listened: with deep sympathy.

The prince assured Dillon that he could one day be ordained as a full-fledged monk. But until the controversy blew over, Dillon would only be allowed to take vows as a novice in the Tibetan tradition. (While there was a ban against monks who belonged to the "third sex," no such ban existed for novices.) Yes, Dillon could enter a monastery in Ladakh, but only if he inhabited the lowest rank, on par with the ten- and twelve-year-old boys who fetched water and served the tea. Kushok Bakula had picked out a monastery where Dillon would be sent: by chance, it was Rizong, the famous monastery of fruit trees and punishments, a place so remote that it bordered on mythological.

Dillon was thrilled. At Rizong, he would witness what so few other Westerners had: Tibetan Buddhism practiced in its most traditional form. The prospect of entering the monastery as a "boy" did not bother him; Dillon saw it as an opportunity to throw off the English arrogance and to learn humility. Indeed, he rather relished the idea of recapturing the experiences he'd been denied as a child—the routine of a strict boarding school and the male camaraderie. Most of all, he looked forward to putting himself under the control of a firm-handed head monk—something like a headmaster in Dillon's fantasy—who acted as a gruff but loving father.

"Rizong!" Dillon declared. "Its strictness . . . would be good for me, as I was much in need of discipline."

In the spring of 1960, Dillon bounced in the back of a jeep as it wound up a steep trail. The air, thin and dry, burned his lungs. Around him stretched a barren landscape of rocks, dust, and dun-colored hills. Dillon had flown into Ladakh on a small, propeller airplane; he carried no possessions besides a robe, a roll of bedding, and a few coins. He did not have enough money for extra food, should he need it at the monastery. He could not speak Ladakhi. He did not even own a pair of decent shoes. Still, he felt lucky. He had managed to get past the border. With tensions in Ladakh so high, Dillon might have been the only Englishman in the entire country. Though Ladakh was tiny and without military muscle, it was a prize because of its enormous strategic value; it occupied a dimple of land between India, China, Tibet, and Pakistan. Within two years, it would become the staging ground for a short war between China and India. Dillon had been able to finagle a travel permit because he knew Prince Kushok Bakula, the Ladakhi leader. His permit would only last for three months.

But for now, he had all he needed. He sat in a jeep that bucked along a dirt track in the mountains, on his way to Rizong. His friend Lama Lobzang had offered to guide him to the monastery, and now the two sat side by side, bumping shoulders. They rode for hours, until the driver dropped them off by the side of the road. For the last leg of their trip, they would hike up a zigzag of steep paths to the monastery.

Dillon struggled to keep up behind Lama Lobzang, tiring quickly in the thin air, shaking rocks out of his flimsy sandals. As he crept along the vertiginous path, inches away from thousand-foot drops, he dared not look away from his feet for even a moment, even at the peaks of Kashmir in the distance, some of the highest and whitest in the world.

Suddenly the path flattened, and he found himself in a glen full of twisted trees—a place almost English in its coziness. They were passing through the apricot orchard—the fruit for which Rizong had become famous.

Soon Lama Lobzang cried out and pointed toward the sky. The monastery nestled in the crotch of two mountain peaks, a labyrinth of whitewashed stairways, terraces, and towers that shone in the sun. Dillon squinted up and thought he saw skulls mounted on sticks. "Were these the mortal remains of long dead monks, keeping a macabre vigil?" he wondered.[1]

"Put your robe on," Lama Lobzang scolded. Dillon hurried to arrange the outer red robe, leaving his left arm bare, folding and draping it the way he'd been instructed, thinking all the while of the rumors about the beatings. However, when he reached the monastery, rather than blandishments Dillon received tea: the yak-butter tea that lubricated every Tibetan get-together. He drank it shyly in a courtyard as red-robed young men crowded around him, examining the stranger who would live among them for the next few months. They spoke Ladakhi; he smiled and gestured.

Now Dillon would present himself to the head monk, called Rizong Rinpoche by his followers; this man would become his guide and spiritual leader while he lived at the monastery. "The thought of the Head Lama himself held no apprehensions," he wrote. "For some time past I had known with certainty that this was the Guru I had been seeking for two years past."[2] Still, "I felt like a small boy being taken to his first boarding school by his father and about to interview the Headmaster."[3]

Dillon and Lama Lobzang threaded their way through the tiny

doors and narrow halls of the monastery and passed through another courtyard. Up close, the skulls affixed to the side of the
monastery turned out to be laughable—carved out of wood and
badly at that. Bit by bit, Rizong was revealing itself to be an entirely
more gentle place than the rumors had let on.

In time Rizong Rinpoche, the head monk, would become one of the
most respected teachers in the Geluk tradition of Tibetan Buddhism; he would be compared to the saint Milarepa because of his
ability to survive three-year stints meditating in caves under the seal
of snowdrifts. But in 1960, Rizong Rinpoche was an obscure monk
in his thirties wearing a patched robe; he could not speak a word of
English—Dillon would end up tutoring him in the language. He
ran the monastery from a room high up in a tower, decorated with
frayed rugs, silk paintings, and a snapshot of the Potala.

That first day, the Rinpoche and Lama Lobzang talked in rapid-
fire Ladakhi while Dillon sat nearby, studying the man who would,
as Dillon put it, "own" him. It's not clear what Lama Lobzang told
the Rinpoche about the frail Englishman who tucked himself into
the shadows of the room. He may well have informed the Rinpoche
that Dillon had once been a woman; but if the guru did know the
secret, he never let on, even after Dillon had taught him enough
English to express the idea.

Rizong Rinpoche had a single eyebrow running across his forehead and dark stubble creeping up his cheeks. "It was interesting
that my Lama should be an ugly man, for in the past in my me-
chanical reactions to people, I had always gone much on appearance, and [judged people by] whether they spoke in cultured accents
and did things that were 'done' [by the English aristocracy] or not.
Here at least was the major reason for my coming to Rizong, to
break down these habits of years that produced criticisms and judg-
ments," Dillon wrote.[4]

He insisted that he should be treated like any other boy who came to the monastery—no concessions for his white skin or advanced age. And so he would take on exactly the same duties that the other novices did, which turned out to be round-the-clock cooking and cleaning in Rizong's kitchen.

"Plumbing is unknown in Ladakh and there were no taps anywhere," he wrote.[5] The place was so filthy that "my main impression was one of blackness, the wood fires having blackened everything in the room, including the monks and the boys."[6]

The first two days Dillon hunched in a corner, watching. No one knew how to communicate with him, and besides, there was Dillon's white skin—none of the monks could see their way to making an Englishman scrub or fetch. When one of the boys called him "sahib," or master, Dillon rose up from the floor and chased him around, boxing him for his mistake. And slowly, this strange, gangly, blue-eyed novice learned the chores by dint of observation. "By the end of a week, I was on the same level as the other [novices], starting before dawn and ending after dusk," scrubbing pots, sweeping the floor, and fetching the endless firewood that fueled the stove.[7] Soon, he became part of the team laboring furiously to keep up with the monastery's schedule of meals and teas and ritual food offerings; he'd picked up enough sign language and Ladakhi words to communicate with the men and boys swirling around him, to share in their hardships and joys.

Dillon found that the oddest mishaps became funny. One morning he was washing a pot, scrubbing it with a fistful of vegetable greens that he'd found on the floor. Later, he watched as the cook seized on the same knot of greens and chopped them up, placing them with a flourish in the bowl he prepared for the esteemed Rizong Rinpoche: the greens had been transformed from floor trash to guru's meal. For his friends in the kitchen, Dillon acted out the "the early history of our Head Lama's lunch, whereat great merriment arose from all but the cook."[8]

He had found here what had eluded him almost everywhere else except at Rooksdown House: simple human kindness, compassionate acceptance, and a deep connection to the people around him. The men and boys at Rizong "made my path easy and I felt perfectly home among them in a way I had never felt among the [Theravada] monks."[9] The work was grinding, food was scarce, and rules were strict, but the men here lived with incredible lightness in surroundings of savage beauty, where one less inch of rainfall a year could mean starvation.

The kitchen staff woke before dawn and worked until nightfall, but their day was punctuated with pranks, good-humored teasing, and laughter. They horsed around, dumping each other in the firewood box; even the head cook got dunked. "No one minded; no one's dignity was hurt," not even Dillon, who had once been so prickly and reserved.[10] One time, he put his hand out to balance himself on what he thought was a wall—it turned out to be a loose piece of wood paneling. In a Charlie Chaplin–like pratfall, he leaned vertiginously, the wall leaning with him. For a moment the busy kitchen turned into a screwball comedy, and then Dillon and the wall crashed to the floor. There was "great merriment at my expense. But the laughter was so spontaneous and good-natured that I felt no embarrassment and joined in it. In those early days I was always doing something that amused my companions."[11] For the first time in his life, he could laugh at himself; something had loosened inside him; some channel to joy had opened up.

But he was always hungry. He'd arrived at Rizong malnourished, and as the weeks went on, he continued to waste away. Some of the monks and the boys who came from nearby villages depended on extra food slipped to them by their families. Dillon had no way to supplement his diet, so he had to make do with what the monastery provided, the broths, small balls of flour, and apricots—not nearly enough. He was also, quite likely, suffering from parasites that prevented him from absorbing nutrients. Dillon's body began to wither and he was bedeviled by his longings for food, particularly sugar, English tea, and meat.

One morning, while he was sitting on the floor among the other kitchen workers, using a twig to try to spear lumps of dough from a watery soup, Dillon was possessed by a gustatory vision so powerful that for a moment it blotted out his surroundings. He saw himself waking up in a bed with crisp sheets in his London men's club. He watched a "tail-coated waiter wheeling a breakfast trolley into my room and handing me the morning paper. As I look at the trolley I see the cornflakes and milk, creamy from the cow . . . and sugar, as much as one wants; under the silver cover is crisp brown bacon and scrambled eggs on fried bread and a rack of toast and marmalade."[12]

Dillon shook his head, and the waiter vanished along with the bacon and eggs, and he found himself once again in the off-kilter kitchen with its filthy floor and dented pots, and his companions sprawled around him—"three dirty boys in ragged dressing-gowns, two smoke-blackened youths, and a couple of [monks] who were breakfasting with us."[13] He'd grown to love the men and boys around him, and they him; this sense of belonging made up for everything else, even the constant hunger. He had friends now. "Their faces were friendly and sincere," he wrote, and "life in the kitchen was happy."[14]

"Tomorrow going Yon Tan," Rizong Rinpoche announced one day to Dillon[15]—the Rinpoche had learned to speak a little English, but not enough to explain what exactly Yon Tan might be.

Dillon guessed it must be a village, but as for where it was or why they might be going, he did not know. The next morning a whole team of monks and kitchen staff set out on an expedition, Dillon included, trekking along a switchback path to a tiny town, nothing but a few houses huddled halfway up a mountain, prayer flags snapping under a blue sky. The kitchen staff set up shop in the local nunnery; they would churn out food as well as a constant supply of tea for the rituals. The monks, for their part, had carried the ancient scrolls from Rizong. These scrolls and their teachings about the void—ideas concerning the nature of nothingness that were central to Tibetan Buddhism—had transfixed Dillon since he'd arrived at the monastery. He'd spied them in the library, but as he was only a novice, he had never been allowed a closer look. The scrolls included the writings of Tsongkhapa, the fifteenth-century founder of the Geluk or "yellow hat" intellectual tradition.

The first morning of their encampment in Yon Tan, the monks unfurled these scrolls and read from them, reciting as quickly as their jaws would move. By afternoon, the weather had drastically changed, so that Dillon shivered in his robes. Lightning flashed. Thunder boomed, drowning out the monks' voices. Dillon caught the eye of one of the monks, Zod-pa, and pointed at the window, indicating his surprise—how had a storm come up so quickly?

Zod-pa left off chanting and looked up at Dillon. Despite the language barrier he managed to explain what was happening: the monks had caused this storm.

Dillon, it seemed, had fallen through the looking glass and landed inside a fairy tale. Years before, he had come across a newspaper story about Tibetan lamas who could brew up storms—a British commission had looked into the phenomenon and determined that, indeed, the monks did seem able to control the weather, although how they managed this the commission never explained. Without knowing it, Dillon had been living among the famous rain-making lamas; but only now did he connect *his* monks with that newspaper article. "There are some things you read of in books but never think could happen to you," he wrote.[16]

Dillon couldn't argue with the results: every morning the sky started blue, but after the monks had chanted about the nature of nothingness for several hours, rain began to peck at the roof and then turned into a torrent. After a few days of this, with the rivers swollen and the streets damp, the monks packed up and left; the crops would be safe.

A few weeks later, Dillon worked up the courage to ask the Rinpoche for permission to use the library and examine the scrolls. The Rinpoche agreed, even though Dillon was technically not supposed to be allowed to study the books until he passed through the higher ordination. Thrilled, Dillon carried one of the scrolls back to his room to pore over it—with a thousand two-and-a-half-foot-long pages it looked more like a bed than a book. He could not believe that he'd finally held such a rarity in his hands. Of course, he could not read it, but he knew that it discussed the nature of the void, of being and nonbeing. He planned to copy down the Tibetan hieroglyphics and translate them later.

"I undid the wrapping carefully and settled down on my mat to see what I could make of it." He pulled out a notebook and began copying down the foreign language as best he could. As he wrote, he found himself scratching—he'd suddenly become terrifically itchy. "I lifted up the pages of the book and ran them through my fingers . . . The whole volume had been the residential quarters of a race of lice, and now, disturbed, they had come out to see what they could find to eat and found me!"[17] Lice from this philosophical tome that discussed the properties of emptiness soon infested the entire room. That night, he could hardly sleep and finally had to pick up his blanket and move to the dining room.

He squashed, flicked, and stomped on bugs—until his guru caught him at it. The Rinpoche told Dillon that such violence went against everything they believed in. Had he forgotten his vows? He had promised to put the comfort of all beings before his own, including lice. From then on, when the Englishman discovered a louse, he escorted it to the window and let it out.[18]

And that's how Rizong enchanted him. Here, you learned not from the vast scrolls swirling with Tibetan letters, but from the bugs that infested its pages; here, rain could be controlled. Here, the wizards who accomplished this feat ate trash from the floor for dinner. Rizong monastery astonished Dillon with its constant paradoxes.

The old Michael Dillon had melted away in the thin air up here, and a new man, the English novice—white skin gone gray with soot—had taken his place. The greatest surprise of all was this: starved, overworked, and filthy, Dillon had finally stumbled across a fragile kind of happiness.

One day, toward the end of his stay at Rizong, Dillon and a small boy set to work unloading sacks of wool from the back of a donkey. "Knowing the limits of my strength after two years of malnutrition, I shouldered a bale of wool as being probably the lighter of the two," Dillon wrote. But once he'd got the load on his back, he found he could not climb the steps up to the monastery; the boy scampered ahead, carrying his bag easily. Dillon collapsed.

He knew he needed medical care and heartier food, but still, he could not bear to leave Rizong. His life was finally taking a shape that made sense to him. He hoped that with a little more money coming in from his recent publishing ventures, he would one day have enough food to settle in at the monastery and live there in some style.

Except that he'd have to leave Rizong. Dillon's Ladakhi friends had tried and failed to negotiate an extension with the Indian authorities so that he could stay in the country. But in the first week of October, his permit ran out, and with tensions high, he could not obtain a new one. "I did not want to go at all! I had been happy here, despite the hard, uncomfortable life, and I felt that I had at last found my home."[19] If the cease-fire between India and China continued, Dillon hoped to return to Ladakh in the spring, when the winter snows melted to open up the perilous road to the monastery. He began to imagine a future in which he could belong to this warren of tiny doorways and halls, with its chink-hole windows that winked with views of blue mountains, and to these men and boys he'd come to love. This could be the place where he finally fit. Standing in a lineup of monks to pose for a photograph, with his shaved head and the sooty fabric of his robe arranged just so, he matched. He—who adored uniforms and teams, who longed simply to be in on the joke instead of the object of it, who hungered to be a face in the crowd— had finally found what he'd been looking for, after so many years.

And he was thrilled with a promise that the Rinpoche had made: when Dillon returned, he would take vows as a monk. Then, as a ranking member of the Rizong community, he would spend his days studying the scrolls in the library—exactly what he dreamed of doing.

On his second-to-last day at Rizong, he visited his guru for what would be the last time, performing a series of customary bows. Somehow, even the ornate bows did not express the depths of Dillon's feelings for this man who had become a second father to him. Only shaking hands would do—that most English of farewells. "I held out my hand. [The Rinpoche] looked at it uncertainly for a moment, as if not quite sure what it was there for, and then grasped it firmly in his own."

"Good-bye, sir, and thank you very much," Dillon said, using the English that he'd taught to the Rinpoche.

And then he returned to the kitchen, reeling with anticipatory homesickness. He knew the kettles and pots so well—each dent, each dimple, each black mark. And yet he might never see them again. "I felt like an old hand, and perfectly at home in my surroundings. And tomorrow I would leave."[20] He was frightened by how much he would miss the smoky smell of the kitchen and the chatter of his friends—and yet how strange to yearn for all this, to miss it, even while it surrounded him.

He gathered up firewood and hauled it back to the kitchen, painfully aware he was performing this familiar task for the last time. "That thought kept recurring and recurring through the whole day. Each time it recurred I tried to banish it again, for this was merely a negative emotion based on self-pity."[21]

The next day, he found himself leading a packhorse down a mountain path, stumbling on numb legs; the dreaded hour of departure had arrived. Above, the kitchen staff waved from the courtyard. "I wondered if I would be able to return, or would the Chinese have invaded before the winter was out."[22] He took a last look back at them before a bend in the road, then he walked on and they were blotted out.

In the fall of 1960, Dillon dragged himself back to Sarnath, where he set up shop once again in the hostel for religious pilgrims. Exiled from Rizong, he would throw himself into writing.

The year before, Dillon had become entranced with the story of Milarepa, a Tibetan saint who had wielded magical powers but gave them up to pursue enlightenment, meditating in a cave for so many years that his skin turned green. Dillon had rewritten the ponderous Evans-Wentz English translation of *The Life of Milarepa*, thinking that he might retool it to be a "racier" story that could be a popular hit in the West. He'd managed to sell the manuscript before he'd left for Rizong, and now he had just received the corrected proofs of the book. The payment would follow soon—enough money to subsist until the spring, when he would try to return to Rizong.

Just as important, he would make his literary debut in England under the name Lobzang Jivaka. (He had added the *Lobzang* in honor of his mentor Lama Lobzang.) Certainly, no one in England would guess at his former identity. "I do not wish my Western name known.

I am heir to a title and have no desire for publicity. Only six people know where I am or what I am doing," he wrote to editor Simon Young, to whom he also refused to reveal his legal name.[23] Not so long ago, Dillon had dreamed of following Sangharakshita's model—to set himself up as an intellectual who funded his spiritual activities with writing, as a man of some importance in the English-speaking Buddhist community. Now that dream was coming true.

With *The Life of Milarepa* finished, he poured out the first few chapters of another book in mere weeks. This one told his adventures in Rizong. Titled *Imji Getsul* (English Novice), the book is more a love story than anything else, a paean to the home he'd found and then lost. He sent three chapters to his editor at the publishing house John Murray. The editor rejected the book. But no matter. A literary agent in London, John Johnson, had offered to take over the representation of Dillon's work; Johnson sent the manuscript around to other houses and Routledge snapped it up. Of course, the book would appear under the name Lobzang Jivaka.

Dillon couldn't mask his true identity entirely. The editors at Routledge required him to explain how the mysterious Jivaka, apparently an English doctor of aristocratic birth, had come to live in India. Certainly, any reader who picked up the book would wonder why a habitué of London men's clubs would go to such lengths to sleep on a flea-bitten mattress in Ladakh. Dillon answered these questions in a mini-autobiography that takes up one chapter of the book. He portrays himself as a former Boy Scout who once dreamed of becoming a "clergyman"; he also implies that he served in the military during the war. In Dillon's version of the story, it is not fear of the tabloid press that sends him hurtling toward India, but instead the emptiness of Western values.

Dillon felt he had no choice but to commit several falsehoods to print in *Imji Getsul*; his inventions, he insists in his memoir, were only "slight twists to the story to mislead those who had known me in England . . . so that idle chatter as to my possible identity would not reach the ears of the press and send reporters flying out to my haven of refuge."[24] But for the scrupulously honest Dillon—a man who had taken religious vows—publishing these untruths must have caused him considerable angst.

Dillon banged out the rest of *Imji Getsul* in the last weeks of 1960 while subsisting on just a few rupees; due to a glitch, he had still not received any payment for his previous book, *The Life of Milarepa*. That winter his hard work, short rations, and chronic malnutrition finally caught up with him: Dillon burned with typhoid fever. Because he had run out of money, he had no choice but to drag himself to the local charity hospital. He watched, helpless, as the staff administered treatments that he, as a doctor, knew would not work. He finally tottered out of the hospital several weeks later, still suffering from jaundice, looking, he wrote, like a "yellow skeleton."[25]

He rallied somewhat in the spring of 1961, still managing to eke out an existence in near destitution at the Maha Bodhi Society hostel, grinding out articles and manuscripts on Tibetan Buddhism that generated just enough income so he could get by. But he never stopped hankering for Rizong. That spring, he mounted a trip to Kashmir to visit Kushok Bakula—the prince who had helped him before—hoping to obtain a travel permit. The plan failed. The Indian officials turned down Dillon's application; they assumed he was a spy.

Dillon's evasiveness about his past contributed to this misunderstanding. In his articles for Indian newspapers, he had presented himself as a British citizen who seemed to have some kind of military service in his background, who had traveled through the contested land of Ladakh, and who refused to give his Western name or any identifying details about himself. A pro-Communist newspaper dedicated a column to sniffing out the truth about Lobzang Jivaka. The paper named him as a member of the British Intelligence, a spy hired by Indian Prime Minister Nehru to keep tabs on the Chinese.

Nehru had to personally step in and insist that he had never hired the mysterious Jivaka.

Dillon's chances of getting into Ladakh seemed slim indeed. Still, he hoped that when the hubbub died down, he might finally win his permit.

And then, in November of 1961, the press inflicted a further insult. A small article appeared in a Hindi-language newspaper, accusing the writer Jivaka of having once been a "lady doctor" and of having had a sex change. Half-starving, huddled in his bare room, Dillon fingered the cheap newsprint, terrified of what would happen next.

He ripped out the article to send it to Sangharakshita, and on a scrap of brown paper he scrawled a note for his teacher that indicates that Dillon regarded Sangharakshita—who'd sent three revealing letters years before—as the initial source of the leak: "You . . . bear the ultimate responsibility. Please send the carbon copy of my autobiography which you have locked up in your trunk, well-packed and registered, just as soon as you can. It will now have to be published."[26] Dillon had readied his manuscript for just this occasion. If the reporters discovered him, he would preempt their story with his own.

And then something strange happened, something Dillon could not have expected, given his weary history with the tabloids: the story generated no attention. None of his friends around town mentioned it. No other newspapers picked it up. Perhaps the story had sunk into obscurity because it had appeared in a dusty little newspaper with few English-speaking readers; whatever the reason, Dillon felt as if he'd miraculously been spared. But his luck could not hold forever.

In the spring, both *The Life of Milarepa* and *Imji Getsul* appeared in British bookstores, and Dillon braced himself for trouble. Surely, some reader would wonder about the secret identity of Lobzang Jivaka and make inquiries. That spring he began to prepare to unmask himself by finishing his autobiography so that it could be

In 1961, when he thought he was about to be outed by the press, Dillon scrawled this note to his former guru. The letter reads: "Dear Sangharakshita, You may like to know that what you once described as a purely Sangha [monastic] matter appears to have been given deliberately to the press . . . You . . . bear the ultimate responsibility. Please send the carbon copy of my autobiography which you have locked up in your trunk, well-packed and registered, just as soon as you can." *From Sangharakshita's private collection, licensed by the Clear Vision Trust*

published. Dillon does not explain how he came to this decision, though of course he had always been a man given to extreme leaps and grand gestures. He would not wait for the press to expose him. He would do it himself.

On May 1, 1962—his forty-seventh birthday—Dillon hunt-and-pecked on a borrowed typewriter in Sarnath. He was finishing up the manuscript that he expected would become a published book, perhaps even a best seller. The manuscript told the story of his girlhood, his earliest homosexual crushes, the testosterone that morphed his body, and trips to Rooksdown to modify his genitals. Dillon held almost nothing back—only his love for Roberta Cowell remained untold. He scribbled corrections into the margins of the manuscript he'd written three years before and added an introduction, decrying the cruelty of the tabloid journalists who had so persecuted him.

He typed "by Michael Dillon" on the cover sheet, then hit the carriage return, and—clack, clack, clack—added "Lobzang Jivaka" underneath. He had come clean. No one could threaten him now. No tabloid could get the scoop. He had lifted the mask himself. When the book came out, he would have to live as a representative of a benighted and despised minority. But he would also, finally, be able to unite all his identities—Laura, Michael, Jivaka—and pull them together into one public persona. He would live more authentically, more freely, than he'd ever dared to before. He packaged up the pages in an envelope and printed out the London address of his agent.

Days later, Dillon headed to Kashmir to renew his efforts to enter Ladakh; once again, he would try to find a way into Rizong. But he never made it there.

At the end of the month, one of Dillon's friends in England received a brief and cryptic note from a Sister Vijara, a British woman who'd been known as Eileen Robinson before she began practicing Theravada Buddhism, and who had befriended Dillon in Sarnath.[27] In the note, she reported that Lobzang Jivaka had died on May 15, 1962, in Dalhousie, an Indian hill station on the border of Kashmir. It's not clear how she knew about his death, and there is no way to ask her. Sister Vijara herself perished in a landslide some years later.

An article in a Buddhist journal elaborated on the facts of Dillon's death: he'd succumbed to illness during a stopover on his way to meet with Prince Kushok Bakula. No one seemed able to say what type of sickness, exactly, had caused the death. According to Sangharakshita, a rumor circulated that Dillon had been poisoned, but there was no solid proof. The details of his death remain an open question.

His body was cremated, in accordance with Buddhist tradition, and the ashes scattered in the Himalayas.

In early summer, the literary agent John Johnson received a plump package in the mail from India; it was, startlingly enough, from his dead client. Inside, Johnson found the autobiographical manuscript, titled "Out of the Ordinary."

Had Dillon survived, he would have become the first person ever to live openly as a female-to-male transsexual. As Harry Benjamin noted, if such a figure had appeared on the scene—a charismatic, well-spoken trans man who could demonstrate what medical science could do to the body—then many more people might have sought treatment. Even posthumously, Michael Dillon might have offered a model, if his book had appeared in print.

But it never did. Dillon's brother, Sir Robert, made it clear that he would do whatever he could to block the publication of the memoir. Indeed, he demanded that John Johnson hand over the manuscript so that it could be burned.[28]

Johnson refused. "Dr. Dillon felt there was no reason why, finally, his story could not be told," Johnson said in a newspaper interview. "He wanted to tell it in his own way, in his own time."[29] Johnson continued to send the manuscript around, but could find no takers. With Sir Robert Dillon and his lawyers ready to cry slander, no publisher dared touch it.

Inside the manuscript, Dillon scrawled notes intended for his future editor—whoever that might be—explaining that the final chapter might have to change, because Dillon was not yet sure how his own story would end. Sangharakshita or someone else might soon trumpet his secret to the rest of the world. If that happened and the tabloids descended upon him, then Dillon would have to change the conclusion of the book to include the story of his downfall. He was willing to identify his tormentors, he wrote in his addendum to the editor. Or, if the editor thought it was wiser, he could leave their names out entirely.

*   *   *.

Sometime in the mid-1960s, Sangharakshita woke up to find his bedroom brimming with light. Over him hovered an apparition. It was his former student Jivaka, who had died several years before. "His hands were joined in supplication, and he was looking upwards with a piteous imploring expression, as if he were begging to be delivered out of the pit."[30] Sangharakshita recited a hundred-word mantra, a chant that is supposed to deliver dying spirits from hell. "As I did so, I saw the letters of the mantra coming out of my mouth, one after another, and forming a chain or garland that went down into the pit and came up out of it in a continuous circular motion. On seeing the garland, Jivaka caught hold of the letters as they ascended and with their help hauled himself out of the pit and disappeared . . . I looked at my watch. It was two o'clock in the morning."[31]

Sangharakshita believes he built a chain of letters that helped to pull Michael Dillon out of perdition. But Dillon's real salvation—his true exit from the pit—would only have come if he'd lived long enough to tell his own story.

In the introduction to the autobiography, he railed against the tabloid magazines that shattered the privacy of people like himself; if only society were more tolerant, he opined, he would not have had to publish this book. He assumed that the book *would* be published and he would face down what he'd always feared most: exposure. In a room in an Indian hostel on May 1, 1962, he typed his two names on a cover sheet—frail onionskin paper, so liable to tear and smudge. Then he carefully pulled that page out of the typewriter and held it up to examine it in a slant of dusty sunlight. At that moment, he believed a new chapter in his life was about to begin. Soon, he would collect his travel permit, cross the Ladakh border, and journey up the switchback paths to Rizong, where he would receive ordination as a full-fledged monk. Most important, he would scatter his secrets before the public; he would reveal what most shamed him. His long struggle to sculpt a perfect self—to control his thoughts, his body, and his image as an Oxford man who'd always been gloriously male—would be over. He would begin a new life as an admitted transsexual and a man with no answers. It might have been the path to enlightenment.

EPILOGUE

WHAT IS THE PART OF US that knows we are male or female? Where is the seed of that certainty? Can it be located in the brain or the body? Throughout the twentieth century, scientists and psychologists have hunted for the part of us that is sexed. In 1937, the *New York Times* crowed that researchers were on the verge of discovering a hormonelike substance in the body, which they nicknamed "it." Whatever "it" was, the substance determined the sex of fetuses in the womb—and provided the script for adult behavior. A University of California biologist had produced charts showing "the secret of 'it'—that high degree of masculinity or femininity that makes man or woman the idol of the opposite sex."[1] Unfortunately, the discovery of "it" never went further than that.

Fifty years later, the hunt was still on. In 1995, a team of researchers in the Netherlands claimed they had identified the seat of gender—in a tiny smudge in the brain stem nicknamed the BSTc. The region is bigger in males than in females; in transsexuals, the pattern is reversed, which seemed to indicate that the feeling of being a man or a woman might originate in this part of the brain. But rival scientists immediately began poking holes in the BSTc theory.

Just how much of the child's brain sex is set at birth has been one of the most hotly contested issues in science. Currently, most researchers agree that crucial elements of our gender identity develop in the womb and just afterward. This supports the accounts of transgendered people, many of whom feel that they were born into their identities and whose earliest memories are of being stuck in the wrong body. "My inner boy showed up early on, when I clobbered the little neighbor boy with my Raggedy Ann doll to get at his Tonka dump truck," according to Eli Wadley; he was born into a female body but eventually transitioned into a man.[2]

Some transgendered people describe growing up with a much more subtle sense of their identity—they experience gender as a tug, a hunch, a cloud of doubt. "I was thirty-nine years old, living as a lesbian, when I first realized I'd probably be happier living as a guy," writes Reid Vanderburgh.[3] Even after hormones and surgery, Vanderburgh never felt resoundingly male. "I gradually came to realize that I had not transitioned from female to male. I had transitioned from female to not female . . . Now I feel I'm neither a man nor a woman, though the limitations of English force me to choose sides. So I'm a guy, much more comfortable with male pronouns than female, but not really feeling like a man."[4]

Few of us can agree on exactly what it means to be male or female, and whether we acquired our gender identity in the womb, at age two, twelve, or forty. Scientists, too, are still far from reaching a consensus about the causes of gendered feelings and behavior. Nor can the medical establishment agree on *how many* people are transgendered. The *Diagnostic and Statistical Manual of Mental Disorders (DSM-IV)* estimates one in thirty thousand biological males in the population and one in one hundred thousand biological females pursue sex changes.[5] Scholar Lynn Conway argues those figures are hopelessly out-of-date. By compiling year-by-year numbers for sex-change surgeries and adding them up, she came up with her own figure: for every twenty-five hundred males in the United States, there is one male-to-female transsexual, according to Conway.[6] She provided no estimate for the incidence of female-to-male transsexuals, however. Indeed, that number is far more elusive. Since the "bottom surgery"—the construction of a penis—is expensive (upwards of one hundred thousand dollars) and prone to infections and other complications, many F-to-Ms do without it. They may rely on testosterone and a double mastectomy to accomplish their switch. This means that many trans men may never be counted. But the real problem is that almost no one is counting: far too little research has been done in this area.

Harry Benjamin defined a transsexual as a person who craves a sex-change operation, who longs specifically for the surgeon's knife to shave and shape his or her genitals; in the 1960s, transsexuality was a syndrome characterized by its cure; you had to have surgery, or want surgery, to be a "transsexual." But by the 1970s, activists had begun to quibble with Benjamin's definition and to look for other ways to talk about gender and its discontents.

In 1968, Virginia Prince performed her own kind of sex change, without bothering to submit herself to screening interviews at a gender identity clinic or going under the knife. She simply began dressing, speaking, and living as a woman full-time and called herself a *transgenderist*. She invented the word to describe people like herself who did not need to change their body to change their sex.

In her extensive writings, Prince laid out a blazingly original view of what makes us masculine or feminine. As she saw it, while all animals are sexed, only people have gender. Like sculpture or tap dance or architecture, gender is a set of flourishes that we use to communicate something about our identity to others, as well as to delight and entertain. Prince practiced her femininity as a high art: in one of her books, she dwells for five pages on the intricacies of ladies' shoes.

The word she'd invented—*transgender*—caught on in the 1970s and evolved into something bigger and more inclusive than what Prince may originally have meant. It became an umbrella term for gender benders of every variety and sexual proclivity. The word resonated with the times. By the 1970s, androgyny had become hip and sexy: glam rockers wriggled across the stage in leather pants and boas; cocaine-thin fashion models vamped in newsboy caps; teenagers in fright wigs waited in line to see *The Rocky Horror Picture Show.* Tiny Tim strummed his ukulele and in baritone and falsetto sang "I Got You Babe"—performing both the Sonny and Cher parts, a veritable duet with himself.

Gender had become a song you made up as you went along, a show tune you lip-synched when it matched the secret beat of your own heart. And the "sex-change operation" had burst out of the hospitals and operating rooms, out of the psychiatrists' offices and the pillbox, and moved out onto the street. What was a man? What was a woman? Those questions would no longer be left to the experts.

ACKNOWLEDGMENTS

First and foremost, I owe effusive thanks to Liz Hodgkinson, the British journalist who pieced together Michael Dillon's story in the 1980s. Liz was kind enough to share incredible Dillon-related documents that she has archived over the years—these resources provided a key to the mysteries surrounding Dillon.

Andrew Hewson also proved to be an enormously generous friend in Britain. He gave freely of his time, advice, office space, and Xerox machine. Without his help, this project would have stalled, and I am hugely grateful to him for his endless favors.

Sangharakshita, Michael Dillon's mentor during his final years, was kind enough to write up his memories for me and answer every question I asked. I was impressed by the vividness of Sangharakshita's recollections and grateful for the care he has taken to record the past. He sent me copies of a number of original letters penned by Dillon; these became a valuable resource as I reconstructed Dillon's years in India.

My friend Scott was able to give me an insider's view of the F-to-M transition and of post-op life. As I worked on this book, we held regular meetings; our conversation meandered from transsexual issues to stuffed French toast, ghost hunting, white tea, and biomass energy. I owe him thanks, then, for his company and his insight into the transgender experience, and also for his brilliant edit of this manuscript.

Dr. Andrew Bamji, the curator of the Harold Gillies archive, sent me photos of Rooksdown along with surgical diagrams that bolstered my understanding of the tube pedicle technique. In addition, Dr. Bamji did me the enormous favor of reading through the bits of the book where I described operations, offering pointers and corrections.

Dr. Ralph Millard, who stood at Gillies's side during the surgeries on both Michael Dillon and Roberta Cowell, interrupted his retirement in Florida to tell me everything he could remember about these landmark medical procedures.

Professor Herbert V. Guenther, a pioneering scholar of Tibetan Buddhism, wrote me several letters in which he described his brief friendship with Dillon during the late 1950s; for this favor, I am tremendously grateful.

In the course of writing this book, I learned that some men become squeamish when they are forced to listen to descriptions of surgeries that involve cutting open the penis. Kevin—my boyfriend, housemate, and officemate—has endured a lot of such talk over the last year and a half. Through it all, he remained a supportive, wise, and impish partner. I am happy that he continues to put up with me, even when I rant about castration techniques for hours on end.

Before I began this book, I wrote a string of articles for John Koch, an editor at the *Boston Globe Magazine*. When I informed John that I wanted to make the switch to "gonzo science writing" he encouraged me to go as gonzo as I liked, allowing me to interview the world's most educated parrot and to investigate a soul-balancing machine stored in a Cambridge auto garage. John also sent me on an assignment to the Harvard Brain Bank, where I had the chance to examine gray matter sliced and diced in every conceivable fashion. That experience proved to be enormously helpful when it came time for me to write about Laura Dillon's job as an assistant in a neurology lab.

My writers group (Tehila Lieberman, Susan Mahler, Karen Propp, Lauren Slater, and Priscilla Sneff) critiqued many chapters of this book, supplied home-decorating tips, and lent ten sympathetic ears.

Liz Canner furnished me with a second home and one of the warmest friendships I have ever known. Even though geography prevents us from fully practicing our Boston marriage, I continue to think of her as my better half.

WMBR's GenderTalk radio show kept me plugged into the transgender scene; hosts Nancy Nangeroni and Gordene MacKenzie do a bang-up job of covering the issues with humor and gusto. Thanks to them, Saturday night is never boring.

When I was about halfway through with this book, I flew to Santa Fe to teach at a creative-nonfiction conference. There I met Natalie Goldberg, who immediately became a friend and inspiration. Over the last year, Natalie has come through for me in all kinds of ways, and I still don't know what I've done to deserve her tremendous largesse.

David McCormick, my agent, remains a trusted adviser and wonderful booster; it was he who helped me turn this idea into a book proposal.

I owe thanks to my editor Colin Dickerman, who provided invaluable advice during the early stages of the writing of this book. Kathy Belden, another Bloomsbury editor, stepped in at the end; she worked tirelessly—and with quiet genius—to turn my manuscript into a far better book. As you read, please try to imagine her penciled comments in the margins and running between the lines. Kathy's ideas hold together my story like those silk threads that, in the old days, used to sew up the bindings of books. She's everywhere in these pages.

I also want to thank everyone in the transgender and gender-free community who offered me advice, insight, and friendship. I was touched by your generosity, and I hope this book proves useful to you.

NOTES

CHAPTER 1: HE PROPOSES

1. Roberta Cowell, *Roberta Cowell's Story* (New York: British Book Centre, 1954), 123.
2. Ibid.
3. Sir Harold Gillies and Dr. D. Ralph Millard, *The Principles and Art of Plastic Surgery* (Boston: Little Brown, 1957), Volume II, 384.
4. Ibid., Volume I, 438.
5. Dillon, "Out of the Ordinary" (unpublished manuscript), 70.
6. Liz Hodgkinson, *Michael Née Laura* (London: Columbus Books, 1989), 89.
7. Ibid., 88.
8. Ibid., 89.
9. Ibid., 90.
10. Michael Dillon, *Self: A Study in Ethics and Endocrinology* (London: William Heinemann Medical Books Ltd., 1946), 51.
11. Ibid., 53.
12. Eric Pace, "Harry Benjamin Dies at 101; Specialist in Transsexualism," *New York Times*, August 27, 1986, D18.
13. Dillon, "Out of the Ordinary," ii.

CHAPTER 2: WHEN THERE'S NO WORD FOR IT

1. Michael Dillon, "Out of the Ordinary," 31.
2. Jamison Green, *Becoming a Visible Man* (Nashville, TN: Vanderbilt University Press, 2004), 7.
3. Michael Dillon, "Out of the Ordinary," 35.
4. Ibid., 44.
5. Alison Oram and Annmarie Turnbull, eds., *The Lesbian History Sourcebook: Love and Sex Between Women in Britain from 1780 to 1970* (London: Routledge, 2002), 197.
6. Dillon, "Out of the Ordinary," 38.

7. Ludwig L. Lenz, MD, *The Memoirs of a Sexologist: Discretion and Indiscretion* (New York: Cadillac Publishing Co., 1954), 404.

8. Ibid., 430.

9. Ibid.

10. Charlotte Wolff, MD, *Magnus Hirschfeld: A Portrait of a Pioneer in Sexology* (London: Quartet Books, 1986), 379.

11. Dillon, "Out of the Ordinary," 33.

12. George L. Foss, "Action of Testosterone Propionate on the Female," *Lancet*, April 30, 1938, pt. 1, p. 992.

13. Ibid., 993.

14. Ibid.

CHAPTER 3: MAGIC PILLS

1. Chandak Sengoopta, "Glandular Politics: Experimental Biology, Clinical Medicine and Homosexual Emancipation in Fin-de-Siècle Central Europe," *Isis* 89, no. 3 (September 1998): 461.

2. Eugen Steinach, MD, *Sex and Life: Forty Years of Biological and Medical Experiments* (College Park, MD: McGrath Publishing Co., 1970), 65.

3. Ibid., 67.

4. Gertrude Atherton, *Adventures of a Novelist* (New York: Blue Ribbon Books, 1932), 555.

5. Harry Benjamin, address given at the twelfth annual Conference of the Society for the Scientific Study of Sex on November 1, 1969. From the collection of the Magnus Hirschfeld Archive for Sexology, Humboldt University, Berlin; no page number given.

6. "Old Age," *Time*, October 22, 1928. Collected on the Time.com Web site in an archive of old issues; no author or page number given.

7. "Voronoff and Steinach," *Time*, July 30, 1923. From Time.com archive.

8. "Slower Aging Seen in Use of Hormone," *New York Times*, September 18, 1935, 25.

9. Oram and Turnbull, *Lesbian History*, 19.

10. Dillon, *Self*, 53.

11. Ibid., 52.

12. Ibid., 55.

13. Ibid., 53.

14. Cowell, *Roberta Cowell's Story*, 33.

15. Ibid., 72.

16. Ibid., 83.

CHAPTER 4: SIR HAROLD'S SCALPEL

1. Dillon, "Out of the Ordinary," 51.

2. Reginald Pound, *Gillies: Surgeon Extraordinary* (London: Michael Joseph, 1964), 26.

3. Ibid., 63.

4. Ibid., 66.

5. Gillies and Millard, *Principles and Art of Plastic Surgery*, Volume II, 371–72.

6. Pound, *Gillies*, 72–73.

7. Ibid., 123.

8. Ibid., 129.

9. Elizabeth Haiken, *Venus Envy: A History of Cosmetic Surgery* (Baltimore: Johns Hopkins University Press, 1997), 35.

10. Dillon, "Out of the Ordinary," 52.

CHAPTER 5: WITH GIRLS ONE HAS TO BE CAREFUL

1. Dillon, "Out of the Ordinary," 54.

2. Gillies and Millard, *Principles and Art of Plastic Surgery*, Volume II, 381.

3. Pound, *Gillies*, 143.

4. Dillon, "Out of the Ordinary," 54.

5. Ibid., 59.

6. Hodgkinson, *Michael Née Laura*, 75.

7. Ibid., 74.

8. Cowell, *Roberta Cowell's Story*, 81.

9. Gillies and Millard, *Principles and Art of Plastic Surgery*, Volume II, 385.

10. Cowell, *Roberta Cowell's Story*, 90.

11. Ibid.

12. Ibid., 96.

13. Ibid., 101.

14. Phone interview with Dr. Ralph Millard, conducted by Pagan Kennedy, September 26, 2005.

15. Gillies and Millard, *Principles and Art of Plastic Surgery*, Volume II, 384.

16. Dillon, "Out of the Ordinary," 70.

17. Dillon, *Self*, 50.

CHAPTER 6: ORCHID

1. Cowell, *Roberta Cowell's Story*, 110.

2. Ibid., 107.

3. Ibid., 116.

4. Ibid., 125.

5. Ibid., 126.

6. Dave King, *The Transvestite and the Transsexual: Public Categories and Private Identities* (Aldershot, England: Avebury, 1933), 54.

7. Hodgkinson, *Michael Née Laura*, 89.

8. Undated document in the collection of Liz Hodgkinson.

9. Gillies and Millard, *Principles and Art of Plastic Surgery*, Volume II, 386.

10. Cowell, *Roberta Cowell's Story*, 127.

11. Ibid., 128.

12. Hodgkinson, *Michael Née Laura*, 87.

CHAPTER 7: A PASSPORT INTO THE WORLD OF WOMEN

1. Gillies and Millard, *Principles and Art of Plastic Surgery*, Volume II, 387.

2. Millard interview.

3. Ibid.

4. Cowell, *Roberta Cowell's Story*, 134.

5. Ibid., 137.

6. Ibid., 150.

7. Ibid., 202.

8. "Got £8,000 for Life Story," *Times* (London), June 20, 1958, 6.

9. Dillon, "Out of the Ordinary," 80.

10. Christine Jorgensen, *Christine Jorgensen: A Personal Autobiography* (New York: Bantam Books, 1968), 167.

11. Ibid., 166.

12. Ibid., 176.

13. Ibid., 77.

14. Ibid., 175.

15. Cowell, *Roberta Cowell's Story*, 161.

16. King, *Transvestite and Transsexual*, 110. Note: Cowell later disputed the figure in an article that ran in the London *Times*. She said she had been paid eight thousand pounds.

17. Liz Hodgkinson, e-mail to Pagan Kennedy, April 19, 2005.

18. Niels Hoyer, ed., *Man into Woman: An Authentic Record of a Change of Sex* (New York: Popular Library, 1953), 89.

19. Sheila M. Rothman and David J. Rothman, *The Pursuit of Perfection: The Promise and Perils of Medical Enhancement* (New York: Pantheon Books, 2003), 30.

20. Hoyer, *Man into Woman*, 136.

21. Ibid., 188.

22. Ibid., 197.

23. Ibid., 190.

24. Cowell, *Roberta Cowell's Story*, 100.

25. King, *Transvestite and Transsexual*, 110.

26. "New Life for Father," *Newsweek*, March 15, 1954.

27. King, *Transvestite and Transsexual*, 112.

28. Ibid., 112–13.

29. Ibid., 113–14.

CHAPTER 8: THE THIRD EYE

1. Dillon, "Out of the Ordinary," 84–85.

2. Ibid., 115–16.

3. Ibid., 116–17.

4. Ibid., 12.

5. T. Lobsang Rampa, *The Third Eye: The Autobiography of a Tibetan Lama*, 2nd ed. (New York: Ballantine Books, n.d.), 75.

6. Ibid., 76.

7. Ibid.

8. Ibid., 77.

9. Christmas Humphreys, *Buddhism* (Harmondsworth, England: Penguin, 1962), 189.

10. Dillon, "Out of the Ordinary," 131.

CHAPTER 9: THE CALLING CARD

1. "Ex-Woman (Now Man) in Line for Peerage," *Baltimore Evening Sun*, May 12, 1958, 3.

2. "Sex Change Confirmed by Doctor," *Baltimore Morning Sun*, May 13, 1958.

3. "Sex Change Makes Briton Heir to Title," *New York Times*, May 13, 1958, 24. For some reason, the *Times* story places Dillon in Philadelphia. In his own account, Dillon does not mention stopping in Philadelphia to speak to the press.

4. "A Change of Heir," *Time* Magazine, May 26, 1958, Time.com archive.

5. Dillon, "Out of the Ordinary," 143.

6. Liz Hodgkinson, *Michael Née Laura*, 137.

7. Dillon, "Out of the Ordinary," 145.

8. "No Jobs for Miss Roberta Cowell," *Times* (London) February 2, 1962, 5.

9. Virginia Allen, entry in Henry Benjamin tribute, *Archives of Sexual Behavior*, Volume 17, Number 1, February 1988, 26–27.

10. Jorgensen, *Christine Jorgensen*, 173.

11. Leah Cahan Schaefer and Connie Christine Wheeler, "Harry Benjamin's First Ten Cases (1938–1953): A Clinical Historical Note," *Archives of Sexual Behavior* 24, no. 1 (1995): 86.

12. Harry Benjamin, MD, *The Transsexual Phenomenon*. Entire book available on the Web at http://www.symposion.com/ijt/benjamin/.

13. Ibid., appendix B.

14. Betty Friedan, *The Feminine Mystique*, chap. 1. Available on the Web at http://www.h-net.org/~hst203/documents/friedan1.html.

CHAPTER 10: BECOMING JIVAKA

1. Sangharakshita, e-mail to Pagan Kennedy, January 29, 2005.

2. Dillon, "Out of the Ordinary," 151.

3. Sangharakshita, *Moving Against the Stream: The Birth of a New Buddhist Movement* (Birmingham, England: Windhorse Publications, 2003).

4. Dillon, "Out of the Ordinary," 130.

5. Sangharakshita, e-mail to Pagan Kennedy, February 1, 2005.

6. Lobzang Jivaka (aka Michael Dillon), *Imji Getsul: An English Buddhist in a Tibetan Monastery* (London: Routledge and Kegan Paul, 1962), 23.

7. Sangharakshita, e-mail to Pagan Kennedy, February, 1, 2005.

8. Dillon, letter to Sangharakshita, from the collection of Sangharakshita.

9. Dillon, letter to Sangharakshita, January 6, 1959, collection of Sangharakshita.

10. Dillon, undated letter to Sangharakshita from "Cell 1, monastery III, the ruins, Sarnath," collection of Sangharakshita.

11. Dillon, letter to Sangharakshita, collection of Sangharakshita.

12. Dillon, *Imji Getsul*, 35.

13. Sangharakshita, e-mail to Pagan Kennedy, January 31, 2005.

14. Dillon, letter to Sangharakshita, January 27, 1959, collection of Sangharakshita.

15. Dillon, *Imji Getsul*, 9.

16. Denma Locho Rinpoche, "My Life in the Land of Snow," Jamyang Buddhist Centre Web site, http://www.jamyang.co.uk/www/teachers/denma_locho_rinpoche.html.

17. Dillon, *Imji Getsul*, 11–12.

18. Herbert Guenther, letter to Pagan Kennedy, January 4, 2005.

CHAPTER 11: A NEW AGE

1. Herbert Guenther, letter to Pagan Kennedy, January 4, 2005.

2. Sangharakshita, e-mail to Pagan Kennedy, February 9, 2005.

3. Thomas Buckley, "A Changing of Sex by Surgery Begins at Johns Hopkins," *New York Times*, November 21, 1966, 1.

4. Ibid.

5. Joanne Meyerowitz, *How Sex Changed: A History of Transsexuality in the United States* (Cambridge, MA: Harvard University Press, 2002), 77.

6. Tom Buckley, *Esquire*, April 1967, 111.

7. Ibid., 113.

8. Ibid., 205.

9. Benjamin, *Transsexual Phenomenon*.

10. Ibid.

CHAPTER 12: RIZONG

1. Dillon, *Imji Getsul*, 22.

2. Ibid., 23.

3. Ibid., 23.

4. Ibid., 44.

5. Ibid., 49.

6. Ibid., 53.

7. Ibid., 54.

8. Ibid., 62–63.

9. Ibid., 76.

10. Ibid., 71.

11. Ibid., 82.

12. Ibid., 61.

13. Ibid.

14. Ibid.

15. Ibid., 101.

16. Ibid., 109.

17. Ibid., 134.

18. Ibid., 135.

19. Ibid., 162.

20. Ibid., 177.

21. Ibid., 178–79.

22. Ibid., 181.

23. Hodgkinson, *Michael Née Laura*, 154–55.

24. Dillon, "Out of the Ordinary," 150.

25. Hodgkinson, *Michael Née Laura*, 177.

26. From the collection of Sangharakshita, note dated November 2, 1961.

27. Sangharakshita, e-mail to Pagan Kennedy, October 4, 2005.

28. "Doctor Chose a Tibetan Life," obituary of Michael Dillon, *Sunday Telegraph*, from the collection of the Gillies archive.

29. Ibid.

30. Sangharakshita, *Moving Against the Stream*, 339.

31. Ibid., 342–43.

EPILOGUE

1. "Says Sex in Future May Be Directed," *New York Times*, January 9, 1937, 19.

2. Morty Diamond, ed., *From the Inside Out: Radical Gender Transformation, FTM and Beyond* (San Francisco: Manic D Press, 2004), 99.

3. Ibid., 104.

4. Ibid., 106–7.

5. American Psychiatric Association, *Diagnostic and Statistical Manual of Mental Disorders*, 4th ed. (Washington, DC: American Psychiatric Association, 1994), 535.

6. Dr. Lynn Conway, "How Frequently Does Transsexualism Occur?" 2001, http://ai.eecs.umich.edu/people/conway/TS/TSprevalence.html.

BIBLIOGRAPHY

BOOKS

American Psychiatric Association. *Diagnostic and Statistical Manual of Mental Disorders,* Fourth Edition. Washington, D.C.: American Psychiatric Association, 1994.

Atherton, Gertrude. *Adventures of a Novelist.* New York: Blue Ribbon Books, 1932.

Benjamin, Harry. *The Transsexual Phenomenon.* Reprint of the book available at http://www .symposion.com/ijt/benjamin/

Colapinto, John. *As Nature Made Him: The Boy Who Was Raised as a Girl.* New York: HarperCollins, 2001.

Coney, Sandra. *The Menopause Industry.* Alameda, Calif.: Hunter House, 1994.

Cowell, Roberta. *Roberta Cowell's Story.* New York: British Book Centre, 1954.

Dalai Lama XIV. *My Land and My People.* New York: Warner Books, 1997.

Diamond, Morty, ed. *from the inside out: Radical Gender Transformation, FTM and Beyond.* San Francisco: Manic D Press, 2004.

Dillon, Michael. "Out of the Ordinary." Unpublished manuscript currently in the possession of Andrew Hewson in London, completed c. 1961.

———. *Self: A Study in Ethics and Endocrinology.* London: William Heinemann Medical Books Ltd., 1946.

Fausto-Sterling, Anne. *Sexing the Body: Gender Politics and the Construction of Sexuality.* New York: Basic Books, 2000.

Friedan, Betty. *The Feminine Mystique,* Chapter 1. Entire book available at http://www .h<->net.org/~hst203/documents/friedan1.html

Gillies, Sir Harold, and Dr. D. Ralph Millard. *The Principles and Art of Plastic Surgery.* Boston: Little, Brown, 1957.

Gilman, Sander L. *Making the Body Beautiful: A Cultural History of Aesthetic Surgery.* Princeton, N.J.: Princeton University Press, 1999.

Green, Jamison. *Becoming a Visible Man.* Nashville: Vanderbilt University Press, 2004.

Haiken, Elizabeth. *Venus Envy: A History of Cosmetic Surgery.* Baltimore: The Johns Hopkins University Press, 1997.

Harrison, Brian. *The History of the University of Oxford: The Twentieth Century.* Oxford: Clarendon Press, 1994.

Hoberman, John. *Testosterone Dreams: Rejuvenation, Aphrodisia, Doping.* Berkeley, CA: University of California Press, 2005.

Hodgkinson, Liz. *Michael Née Laura.* London: Columbus Books, 1989.

Hoyer, Niels, ed. *Man into Woman: An Authentic Record of a Change of Sex.* New York: Popular Library, 1953.

Humphreys, Christmas. *Buddhism.* Harmondsworth, England: Penguin, 1962.

Jivaka, Lobzang (a.k.a. Michael Dillon). *Imji Getsul: An English Buddhist in a Tibetan Monastery.* London: Routledge and Kegan Paul, 1962.

Jorgensen, Christine. *Christine Jorgensen: A Personal Autobiography.* New York: Bantam Books, 1968.

King, Dave. *The Transvestite and the Transsexual: Public Categories and Private Identities.* Aldershot, England: Avebury, 1933.

Lenz, Ludwig L. *The Memoirs of a Sexologist: Discretion and Indiscretion.* New York: Cadillac Publishing Co., 1954.

Meyerowitz, Joanne. *How Sex Changed: A History of Transsexuality in the United States.* Cambridge, MA: Harvard University Press, 2002.

Oram, Alison, and Annmarie Turnbull, eds. *The Lesbian History Sourcebook: Love and Sex Between Women in Britain from 1780 to 1970.* London: Routledge, 2002.

Pound, Reginald. *Gillies, Surgeon Extraordinary.* London: Michael Joseph, 1964.

Rampa, T. Lobsang. *The Third Eye: The Autobiography of a Tibetan Lama.* New York: Ballantine Books, second edition (no date given).

Rothman, Sheila M., and David J. Rothman. *The Pursuit of Perfection.* New York: Pantheon Books, 2003.

Rubin, Henry. *Self-Made Men: Identity and Embodiment Among Transsexual Men.* Nashville: Vanderbilt University Press, 2003.

Rudacille, Deborah. *The Riddle of Gender: Science, Activism, and Transgender Rights.* New York: Pantheon Books, 2005.

Sangharakshita. *Moving Against the Stream: The Birth of a New Buddhist Movement.* Birmingham, England: Windhorse Publications, 2003.

Steinach, Eugen. *Sex and Life: Forty Years of Biological and Medical Experiments.* College Park, MD: McGrath Publishing Co., 1970.

Wilson, Robert A. *Feminine Forever.* New York: Pocket Books, 1968.

Wolff, Charlotte. *Magnus Hirschfeld: A Portrait of a Pioneer in Sexology.* London: Quartet Books, 1986.

ARTICLES

"A Body to Match the Mind." *Time*, Dec. 2, 1966.

"A Change of Gender." *Newsweek*, Dec. 5, 1966.

"Bargain Breasts and Noses: British Head Abroad for Nips, Tucks." Bloomberg.com, Sept. 9, 2005.

"Capric Candidate," *Time*, Oct. 17, 1932. Time.com archive.

"Doctor Chose a Tibetan Life." Michael Dillon obit in the *Sunday Telegraph*, June 24, 1962.

"Ex-Woman (Now Man) in Line for Peerage." *Baltimore Evening Sun*, May 12, 1958.

"Feminine Forever." *Newsweek*, April 3, 1967.

"Goat Glands & Sunshine." *Time*, Nov. 16, 1931. Time.com archive.

"Got £8,000 for Life Story." *London Times*, June 20, 1958.

"No Jobs for Miss Roberta Cowell." *London Times*, Feb. 2, 1962.

"Old Age." *Time*, Oct. 22, 1928. Time.com archive.

"Sex Change Confirmed by Doctor." *Baltimore Morning Sun*, May 13, 1958.

"Sex Change Makes Briton Heir to Title." *New York Times*, May 13, 1958.

"Slower Aging Seen in Use of Hormone." *New York Times*, Sept. 18, 1935.

"Voronoff and Steinach." *Time*, July 30, 1923. Time.com archive.

"What Am I Doing?" *Time*, Feb. 12, 1940. Time.com archive.

Allen, Virginia. Entry in Henry Benjamin tribute. *Archives of Sexual Behavior*, vol. 17, no. 1, Feb. 1988.

Benjamin, Harry. Address given at the 12th Annual Conference of the Society for the Scientific Study of Sex on November 1, 1969. www2.hu-berlin.de/sexology/gesund/archiv/remini.htm

Buckley, Thomas. "A Changing of Sex by Surgery Begins at Johns Hopkins." *New York Times*, Nov. 21, 1966.

Buckley, Tom. "The Transsexual Operation." *Esquire*, Apr. 1967.

Conway, Lynn. "How Frequently Does Transsexualism Occur?" 2001. Unpublished paper available at http://ai.eecs.umich.edu/people/conway/TS/TSprevalence.html

Foss, George L. "Action of Testosterone Propionate on the Female." *The Lancet*, Apr. 30, 1938, part I.

Fulton, John F. Untitled review of *Charles-Edouard Brown-Sequard: a nineteenth century neurologist and endocrinologist*. *Isis*, vol. 39, no. 3, Aug. 1948.

Hass, Nancy. "Now on the Web: Plastic Surgery for Voyeurs." *New York Times*, Sept. 19, 1999.

Locho, Denma. "My Life in the Land of Snow." Jamyang Buddhist Centre Web site, http://www.jamyang.co.uk/www/teachers/denma_locho_rinpoche.html

Loory, Stuart H. "Surgery to Change Gender." *New York Times*, Nov. 27, 1966.

Pace, Eric. "Harry Benjamin Dies at 101; Specialist in Transsexualism." *New York Times*, Aug. 27, 1986.

Pharr, Suzanne. "Homophobia: A Weapon of Sexism." The SIECUS Report (Sex Information and Education Council of the U.S.), vol. 21, no. 3, Feb./Mar. 1993.

Reis, Elizabeth. "Impossible Hermaphrodites: Intersex in America, 1620–1960." *Journal of American History*, Sept. 2005.

Schaefer, Leah Cahan. "Memorial for Harry Benjamin." *Archives of Sexual Behavior*, vol. 17, no. 1, Feb. 1988.

Schaefer, Leah Cahan, and Connie Christine Wheeler. "Harry Benjamin's First Ten Cases (1938–1953): A Clinical Historical Note." *Archives of Sexual Behavior*, vol. 24, no. 1, 1995.

Sengoopta, Chandak. "Glandular Politics: Experimental Biology, Clinical Medicine, and Homosexual Emancipation in Fin-de-Siècle Central Europe." *Isis*, vol. 89, no. 3, Sept. 1998.

Shukman, Henry. "Friends of the Western Buddhist Order." *Tricycle*, Summer 1999.

Stryker, Susan, ed. "Lou Sullivan in His Own Words." *FTM Newsletter*, Spring 2005.

Tackla, Michelle. "Cultural Turn, Turn, Turn," *Cosmetic Surgery Times*, Jan. 1, 2004.

INTERVIEWS AND CORRESPONDENCE

Phone interview with Dr. Ralph Millard, Sept. 26, 2005

Liz Hodgkinson, e-mail correspondence with author

Herbert Guenther, letters to author

Sangharakshita, e-mail correspondence with author

ARCHIVES

Michael Dillon and Roberta Cowell letters and documents from the collection of Liz Hodgkinson

Michael Dillon letters from the collection of Sangharakshita

INDEX

Note: Page numbers in *italic* refer to illustrations.